Axel Vervoordt

Stories and Reflections

Axel Vervoordt
Stories and Reflections

In collaboration with
Michael James Gardner

Flammarion

Axel Vervoordt at home.

For May
For Boris and Michael, Dick and Marleen
For my grandchildren, Kay, Yasmine, and John
For family, friends, mentors, and artists
who are *tariki hongan* for me

Author's Note

In the process of creating this book, I relied upon
my memory of many different experiences in my life.
I recounted the stories to my son-in-law in English,
which is not my native language. We consulted family
members and others who appear in these stories to read
drafts, provide edits, or offer their own accounts of the
events as we lived them. We researched facts and details
when we could. I have changed the names in some
cases or omitted them altogether. I occasionally left
out certain details, but only when that didn't change
the purpose or emotional truth of the story and why
I wanted to share these memories with you.

—Axel Vervoordt

Contents

Inherited Happiness

Life can change in an instant.

My mother was seventy-nine when she came to an opera gala at the castle outside of Antwerp where my wife May and I live. She loved the performances and the dinner that followed and she stayed well past midnight. Her friend Marcelle invited her for breakfast the next morning. She didn't feel well after breakfast, so she phoned the clinic. They sent an ambulance to bring her to the hospital. I was working in Brussels when I got the news. I raced to be with her. The doctors told me that she had a heart condition and might not recover.

She was in a deep sleep when I saw her. I thought it was the end. The thought of losing her so suddenly was too much to bear.

Slowly, she opened her eyes.

"Mani, what happened?" I asked.

"I don't know, son. I think it's happiness."

"What do you mean?"

"All of your friends were so kind to me last night. It was too much for my old heart."

"Are you sure?" I asked.

"Of course I'm sure," she said. "Pure happiness. It runs in the family. My own grandfather died when the king of Belgium gave him a medal. The king pinned the decoration to his lapel and he was so happy that he just dropped dead."

My mother could have said the evening was too exciting, the food too plentiful, or that she slept too little. Any cause could have been to blame and I would have believed it. But, it was typical of her to be positive. She was grateful even when times were tough. She never paid attention to what she lost—only to what she gained.

She taught me that you can win in life and you can lose, but ultimately, you have a choice. Winners are the people who take their wins and losses in both hands, but they continue playing with only the winning side.

Something happened recently that reminded me of the conversation I had with my mother in the hospital years ago.

Last year, May and I were preparing to go to the opera in Antwerp when I felt something strange in one of my eyes. I called an eye doctor who is a close friend of the family and explained my blurry vision. He suggested that we continue with our evening plans, but we made a consultation appointment after the performance. He told me to call him back in the meantime if anything changed.

Axel as a newborn with his parents.

We arrived at the theater and took our seats. Suddenly I couldn't see the stage. In one eye, I saw flashing lights and then nothing at all. Everything had gone black.

I called the doctor again. He told us to come directly to the clinic.

Riding in the car, I thought I had gone blind. In my mind, I planned to reorganize my life. I would make changes at home so that I could move easily from room to room. I would work, but travel less. I would spend more time listening to music. I found comfort in thinking I could still do what I loved.

I didn't panic, because I didn't see the situation as a problem.

I was treated quickly, and my vision was restored.

But it got me thinking. I wondered why—in the midst of uncertainty—I had remained calm.

Throughout my life, I've been known as a dealer, designer, taste-maker, antiquarian, architect, and curator. But to be honest, I don't like labels.

When people ask what I do, I can't say definitively because my job changes all the time. My vision and way of seeing the world defines my work. I edit with my eyes. My task is to eliminate the unnecessary and uncover the essence of things, to give objects a better place, and create spaces that make people happy.

Over the years, I've told many stories about my life in conversations with family and friends, often during dinner parties. My storytelling evolved naturally, and eventually I was encouraged to put the stories on paper. In the past, I've written books about art, architecture, lifestyle. I like to share my work and practices. But this book became something different.

Portrait of Axel's mother Elsa—whom friends
and family call Mani—at her eightieth birthday party.

It's not a memoir or an autobiography—it's not my entire life story told in detail. I simply started by making a list of memories and little stories. Some took place many years ago. Some were key events, big and small, and others were stories that made me laugh, think, and reflect.

They're a collection of moments I keep coming back to.

I recounted my childhood and realized things that I hadn't known about my parents and what I might have inherited from them. In the process, some stories showed me how I became myself. Of course, not everything that happened is in this book. Memory is selective. It works by omission.

Throughout the process of writing and editing, one purpose remained clear: I wanted to search for the emotional truth in the stories I had to tell.

Like my mother, I noticed my preference for pride in place of pity.

It's one-sided. I remember the excitement and good times.

When there was a little lesson I learned, like happiness, I wanted to share it with you. These are my reflections.

Madame Augusteynen

I was seven when I started selling flowers to my neighbors. I often walked with my father to see the horses in the meadows of the park at Rivierenhof. I loved the first yellow wildflowers in spring, and so I dug a few out of the ground. I wanted to bring the beauty of what I saw home with me.

When we got to our house, I put the flowers in small pots and presented them for sale to our neighbors. Our neighbor, Madame Augusteynen, bought everything I had and quickly became my best client.

A few days after her first purchase, she gave me a new task.

Every morning, she would give me money to buy a fresh round loaf for her at the neighborhood bakery. The first time I walked back carrying the warm bread in my hands, I peeled off a small, delicious piece of crust and put it in my mouth. I had changed the bread's perfect shape, so I peeled a bit from the opposite side. I thought she wouldn't notice if I peeled small pieces all the way around. I walked back to her house—peeling and eating, eating and peeling—until my cheeks were full.

I arrived at her house and rang the doorbell. The loaf was unrecognizable from the one that just left the shop. She was so enthusiastic with the delivery that she gave me a hug and kissed my cheeks. It made me happy to see how happy she was.

The next morning, my job was the same.

Although I was afraid that she'd noticed my trick, I couldn't resist the flaky crust. I arrived at her door—she thanked me again with a hug and a kiss.

I don't remember now how many days I delivered bread for her, but she never, ever complained.

Madame Augusteynen lived a long life and always remained a friend. I visited her once years later and she had a question for me.

"Axel, do you remember when you were little and I asked you to deliver my bread?"

"Of course I do...."

"Wasn't that a strange baker—to make bread with so many holes?"

She winked at me and laughed.

We hugged and she kissed me on the cheek.

The first yellow flowers and trips to the bakery, despite my naïveté, were on her terms. You receive what you accept. She wanted me to know that.

The Story of My Life

I owe part of my ambition to someone I've never met. I learned about him through a painting that hung in our family's home. The man I saw in the painting intrigued me. I asked my parents to tell me more about him.

The seated man was my great-grandfather on my father's side. He was an engineer who built a successful gas company in Antwerp in the nineteenth century. He was known as a generous man, not only in our family, but in the community as well. He used his company's profits to develop a few streets in the suburbs to build houses for the employees. During times of conflict or upheaval, he paid their salaries and continued providing housing for the staff even when the company's operations were shut down.

His daughter—my grandmother—married an army colonel. It was a respected job, but he received no salary, so my great-grandfather gave the couple property as a wedding present so they would receive rental income. The gift included land and several houses on a little street.

My great-grandfather lived in a castle, which was a nineteenth-century country house built in a typical medieval style. In his free time, he devoted himself to the arts. He invited well-known musicians and artists of his day—like Charles Verlat, De Beuckelaer, and others—to join him at home for parties and salons. When I heard this, I imagined what this grand atmosphere was like. I pictured long afternoons filled with spirited conversations in which knowledge was shared. I thought of the great food and wine that would be served while the guests engaged in fast-moving dialogues about art, science, philosophy, music, business, and the future. I dreamed of a creative atmosphere of ideas.

I was inspired by every detail of his life, but then the story took an unexpected turn.

One day, my great-grandfather saw his brother fall off a horse. He had always encouraged his brother to go horse riding, and when he saw the violent fall he thought his brother was dead. He had a heart attack from the shock.

My great-grandfather died—his brother survived.

His widow—my great-grandmother—remarried her handsome coachman. With access to the family's money, the coachman became a gambler and lost many bets on horses and pigeons. After a period of time elapsed, the fortune was gone. All that was left were the properties given to my grandmother as a wedding gift.

My great-grandfather's story fascinated me. I wanted to be like him. I dreamed of restoring the atmosphere he created. I wanted

Painting by De Beuckelaer of a young violin
player with Axel's great-grandfather, who enjoyed
the company of artists and musicians.

to live in a castle and be friends with artists and musicians. I dreamed of an interesting life that could be shared with others.

The castle in Rosenhof where he lived is no longer standing. In fact, I never saw it. The property was developed into several smaller streets, and today the area is full of homes.

When my father passed away from a heart attack, my mother didn't want to remain in the house they shared and to be surrounded by so many memories. She began to give us objects from our family home. I asked my sister Hedwige if I could have the portrait of our great-grandfather. I told her that she could have any part of the inheritance she wanted. I wouldn't argue. The one thing I wanted more than anything was the painting. It helped me to create a story of my life.

Sliding Doors

My sister Hedwige is eight years older than me. Our parents tried to have another baby after she was born, but there was a heart-breaking period during which my mother had numerous miscar-riages. The doctors said she couldn't have more children. If she did, it would be dangerous. When I was born eight years later, it must have been more than a surprise.

As a boy, I used to ask Hedwige, "Are you sure they wanted me?"

She didn't even want to hear the question.

"Of course you were wanted!"

When I was born, they gave me the name Axel, which was rare in our town. My mother was enchanted by *The Story of San Michele*, an autobiography written by the Swedish doctor Axel Munthe. She loved the romantic story about Capri where Munthe made his home in a ruined villa that he magnificently restored.

She loved to read about his art collection, his medical practice, his ideas about health and society, and his philanthropic work.

My grandmother also loved the name Axel, because she knew all of the stories about Hans Axel von Fersen—a count and general in the Royal Swedish Army—who had a passionate love story with Marie Antoinette.

In 2008, I saw an exhibition about the life of Marie Antoinette at the Grand Palais in Paris, designed by my friend Robert Carsen. I was deeply touched to see a letter she had written to Hans Axel von Fersen dated June 29 (my birth date) in the year 1791.

Mon cher Axel,

J'existe mon bien aimé et c'est pour vous adorer...

Adieu, le plus aimé des hommes...

Je vous aimerai jusqu'à la mort.[1]

My mother and I always had a special bond. She was my greatest champion. When I was seven, my sister brought home some clay that she needed for a special project at school. I attended a Jesuit elementary school and the teachers had recently taught us the story of Christ. They said that although he was a king and savior, he was beaten and nailed to a cross where he died.

I couldn't believe it. I thought if he was a king then he shouldn't suffer. The story made me deeply sad.

I went to my sister's room and took her clay. I made a portrait of Christ the way I saw him. I carved the face with the features of

---

[1] My dear Axel, I exist my beloved in order to adore you...
Farewell, most loved of men... I will love you until I die.

Axel's sculpture of Christ that he made at age seven.

a smiling king. I would have said that he was smiling like Buddha, but then I had no idea who Buddha was. I showed the clay figure to my mother.

She was so proud that she took the sculpture to school to show the teachers. The Jesuits shared her enthusiasm and wanted to have a hundred copies made to hang in all of the classrooms.

My mother offered to find someone who could assist in the reproduction.

She'd heard there was someone who worked at the art academy in Antwerp and could make molds and copies. She went to visit the artist at her home at Hendrik Conscience Square.

My mother looked at the artist's work and asked her for help.

"I will do it," the artist said. "But I have to finish it before I leave."

"Where are you going?" asked my mother.

"I'm planning to travel around the world."

"Wonderful! How long will you be gone?"

"That depends. I'm selling my house to raise funds for the trip."

My mother fell in love with the story. "Maybe I'd like to buy your house," she said. She negotiated the price, and without discussing it with my father, she made an offer to buy the sixteenth-century house. The artist could take her trip.

It was the first house my mother bought in Antwerp's historic center and the beginning of our family's story of acquiring and restoring old houses. Life is a series of sliding doors. My mother's impulsive initiative eventually led me to the Vlaeykensgang, which would change my life.

Over time, I went with my mother to follow the house's restoration. In those days, the city was tearing down many old houses around City Hall to make social housing apartments for under-privileged citizens. It was a worthy project, but it came at the expense of destroying buildings tied to Antwerp's grand medieval history, when the city was one of the most important in Europe. My mother was sad to witness this and tried to save what she could.

My father controlled our family's finances and, although he gave her the money to buy the houses, he didn't even want to look at them. He didn't like that part of town. He always said, "Why do you even want to go there?"

My mother was excited every time we went to the neighbor-hood. She took responsibility for the projects and, once the reno-vations were complete, she'd find artists who were looking for a home and studio and she offered them cheap rent.

In a way, she did the same work that the city was doing to cre-ate affordable housing, but she did it in her own unique manner. Over the years, she even bought a few more houses around the corner from the first house.

After several years, my father began to realize that my moth-er's impulses were good investments. She discovered historic houses, restored them, and saved the neighborhood's creative character, which eventually raised their long-term value.

I loved going with my mother to see the houses. She went into every little shop that we passed to find things that she liked. She introduced me to friends and artists. Through the people we met, I took lessons in sculpture and painting. It was the beginning of my lifelong, self-taught education in art.

Across the street from the artist's house that she had bought, we met a woman named Nadya Levi, a dealer who specialized in tribal art and sculpture. As we became friendly with Nadya, she asked if she could make my portrait in clay. I still have it today and it reminds me of those days.

In my early teens, I went to work part-time in Nadya's shop during school holidays. She taught me a lot about tribal and Egyptian art. With the small funds I earned from the job, I wanted to buy my own pieces from Nadya and other dealers. I explored the neighborhood and visited shops and exhibitions.

Once, Nadya sold a sarcophagus and mummy to a client in Paris. She asked me to ride along in her small car for the delivery across the border from Belgium to France. The mummy filled the car's hatchback and I thought every bump in the road would break the body in two.

My experiences in Nadya's shop were important in developing my eye. She showed me how Picasso and Giacometti used tribal art as inspiration in their work. Ever since, I've been fascinated by the connections between artists living in different worlds—it was the beginning of my search for universal links across geography, between genres, and throughout time.

The Vervoordt family at the Belgian seaside.
From left to right: Axel, Jos, Mani, and Hedwige.

Lilies of the Valley

I was nine when my grandmother died in May 1956. Her house was quiet when my sister, parents, and I visited. Her entire bed was completely covered with fresh lilies of the valley. Whenever I smell their sweet scent, even in a luxury perfume, my mind drifts to the past and I think only of my grandmother's deathbed.

She was an intellectual with a great sense of humor and came from a well-to-do family. Throughout her life she didn't work. When she was about forty, the doctors said she had a heart condition, so until she passed away in her eighties she spent most days at home reading the classics and sharing the knowledge of what she found in books with those around her.

My grandmother's first husband died young. Her second husband was nineteen years her junior and, although it didn't look like a good match in the beginning, they liked each other. Over time though, they started to live separate lives. My grandfather liked going out and he earned a bit of a reputation for it.

I liked my grandfather, because he was my father's foil.

While my father was strict and sensible, my grandfather was free and generous. He lived life in his own way. It seemed he had no rules at all.

One day, I was preparing to go camping for two weeks with the Boy Scouts. My mother helped me pack and my father gave me some spending money. Before leaving, they sent me to my grandfather to say goodbye.

I arrived at his house and the first thing he said was:

"How much money did your father give you for the trip?"

I pulled the money from my pocket and opened my hand.

"This much."

"That's impossible! How dare he send you away for two weeks with nothing? Take this, my boy."

He stuffed a wad of cash in my hand.

"It's a present—don't tell your parents. Buy plenty of drinks and ice cream. You've got to be nice to make nice friends."

I offered snacks to everyone.

The Scout leader was furious when he called my parents at home.

"This is a camp, not a resort. You should never give that much money to a child. It sends the wrong message."

My parents were totally confused.

"How much did you give him?" my mother asked my father.

"He's exaggerating. I didn't think it was that much."

It always stayed our secret.

I was sixteen years old when my grandfather died in 1963. Since then, I haven't been afraid of death. He turned a sad moment into one of acceptance. It was the most moving experience I've ever had. We were hand-in-hand as I sat next to his hospital bed. I looked deep in his eyes. There was no tension in his face. When he closed his eyes and took his last breath, I didn't let go of his hand.

Answer to My Tenderness

Throughout my childhood, we never moved. We lived in the same house on the border of Borgerhout close to Rivierenhof, just outside of Antwerp. My mother always wanted to move, and she often tried to convince my father to support her idea.

"Let's take your horses and move to the country," she said.

She pushed and pushed until my father relented. Whenever he was ready to buy a house or a piece of land, she would suddenly change her mind.

"I'm happy where we are," she said. "Let's stay put."

My father gave up. She was quite clever, because she knew exactly how far she could go without getting a result, which, in the end, she didn't truly want. She was a dreamer who enjoyed the process of making plans. I'm different. I dream of something and I won't stop until I realize it. Once my mother could realize her dreams, she didn't want to pursue them anymore. It wasn't her style to play games, although I know it seems like that's exactly what she was doing. Perhaps she's the only one who knew what her real motivation was.

In our house, my mother's taste was avant-garde. When everyone we knew had polished parquet floor, she wanted terracotta.

She wanted bright, white walls to give us light in the winter. She filled the house with Caucasian carpets, and, when winter turned into spring, she took them all away. She was inspired by Jacques Couëlle's work in Sardinia. She changed the interior all the time. My father hated it, but he always adapted. There was only one rule: she never moved his wing chair, which was next to the fireplace.

The house where we lived was cozy. My mother created a welcoming atmosphere that everyone felt as soon as they walked in. Whether the client who bought my father's horses was a prince or a farmer, we sat at one table together and everyone was at ease. My parents made it work.

On two separate days each week, my mother hosted two groups of friends for afternoon tea. These afternoons filled our house with music, conversation, and laughter. She dressed immaculate tables with china and small vases filled with colorful flowers. She had a knack for simple decorations that were full of charm. Inevitably, one of her girlfriends ended up playing the piano and everyone sang along.

The two groups of friends had contrasting musical styles. One group preferred Chopin and the other liked Rachmaninoff. One of my mother's friends was an excellent piano player and she could play by ear. She would visit the cinema and then come to

Joyce DiDonato performs a private concert
at the castle of 's-Gravenwezel for Inspiratum.

our house and play from memory a song that she had just heard at the movies. I always listened in awe.

My mother invited her cousin Rosa to join in from time to time. Although there was a big age gap between her and my mother—Rosa was much older—they had a connection.

Rosa was elegant and kind, but there was something sad about her. Like many others, she lost a lot in the 1930s. For many years after, she lived on a small budget, but managed with style. In my memory, she always wore the same outfit—her last diamond brooch pinned to a well-cut tweed suit.

Rosa's husband suffered from depression, and the weekly visits to our house offered joy during dreary days. Whenever there was even a small sum to spare, she bought a ticket to the opera. She loved the German composer Richard Wagner. A highlight of her year was going with her son to the Bayreuth Festival. She talked about it for the rest of the year until she went back again. Rosa also played the piano well and she often played Wagner arias or romantic pieces from productions she had recently seen.

Despite her kindness, her visits became too heavy for my mother on certain afternoons. Rosa was smart, and occasionally her philosophizing became tiring. When that happened, my mother wasn't shy about disappearing into another room to read a book. Sometimes she even hid in the bathroom. When Rosa was alone in the sitting room, she went to the piano and took a seat in front of the keys.

One afternoon, after she had recently seen *Samson and Delilah* by Camille Saint-Saëns, she sat down at the table and played "Mon cœur s'ouvre à ta voix."[2] It was an aria she played over and over again throughout the years. I listened from another room as the sound filled the house.

Years later, I was in my forties when I heard a Maria Callas performance of "Mon cœur s'ouvre à ta voix" and the lyrics stung my heart with a longing for those days.

Mon cœur s'ouvre à ta voix,	"My heart opens to your voice
comme s'ouvrent les fleurs	like the flowers open
aux baisers de l'aurore!	to the kisses of the dawn!
Mais, ô mon bienaimé	But, oh my beloved,
pour mieux sécher mes pleurs,	to better dry my tears,
que ta voix parle encore!	let your voice speak again!
Dis-moi qu'à Dalila	Tell me that you are returning
tu reviens pour jamais	to Delilah forever!
Redis à ma tendresse	Repeat to my tenderness
les serments d'autrefois,	the promises of old times,
ces serments que j'aimais!	those promises that I loved!
Ah! réponds à ma tendresse!	Ah, answer to my tenderness!"

Answer to my tenderness. The promises of old times. Callas's voice filled the air with a heat that seared my heart. It never occured to me as a boy, but, years later, I was shaken by the realization of what I couldn't grasp at the time. Rosa returned to her story in music—how dazzling was her despair.

---

[2] "My heart opens to your voice."

Influenced by the afternoons with my mother and her friends, I loved classical music and opera as I grew up. When my school friends were obsessed with the Beatles, I listened to Beethoven and tried to name concertos by the first three notes. I didn't like jazz, either. As I got older, my sister's husband Walter introduced me to jazz and helped me to develop an appreciation that has deepened over the years.

Like other families, it was a tradition in our house to have Sunday lunch. My mother's specialties were roast beef served with peas or croquettes, and roasted chicken and vegetables. There was always great wine served with the meal.

After lunch, we listened to *Bel Canto*, a famous radio program. There was often a debate about who was the better soprano, Maria Callas or Joan Sutherland. In our family, we liked Callas, but it was fascinating to listen to the debate about the color and flourish of Sutherland's voice versus Callas's range and interpretations. When the clock struck two, my father insisted on a siesta and everyone had to be quiet. He fell asleep in the living room.

One afternoon, we'd forgotten to lower the volume on the radio as the debate ended. Suddenly, my father yelled from the sofa: "I can't hear! Turn it up. Is it Callas or Sutherland?"

When I became older, I wanted to restore the atmosphere of making music at home with friends. I created Inspiratum with Koen Kessels to share a passion for music with other admirers. Rather than big concert halls, we wanted to bring music back to a more human scale by producing concerts in intimate, private spaces in

At Kanaal, Katia and Marielle Labèque perform
a Bach concerto for two fortepianos for Inspiratum.

order to have close contact with the instruments and world-class musicians, like Joyce DiDonato, Renaud and Gautier Capuçon, and Katia and Marielle Labèque.

My passion for music started during those afternoons at home as a child with my mother and her friends. I understand now that I inherited joy from those days. Once you have that, you want to share it.

How to Get a New Fur Coat

My father was a horse trader. You could say horses were also his hobby, but in fact they were his life. He was always working, thinking, and talking about horses. When he was a child at boarding school, he heard the sound of horses in the fields next to his school. His curiosity sent him climbing over a stone wall to take a look. He started young in the business and never stopped.

My mother liked horses well enough, but she wasn't involved in his work. She wasn't business-minded. Every month, she received an allowance from my father to organize the household. It was how things were done. She had the capability to manage finances, but it didn't interest her. She preferred spending to managing. My mother's interests in historic properties were good investments, but it wasn't a strategy. She acted with her heart.

My father, on the other hand, was a businessman. He often thought he was losing money, even if it wasn't true. If he planned to earn a specific profit from a certain deal or by selling a horse, if it was one cent less than what he had in mind, it wasn't gaining. It was losing.

He said, "Oh, I lost again."

He often bought one hundred horses at once. They came by train or boat from Poland, England, or Ireland and arrived in Essen, a small Belgian town near the Dutch border. Once they were unloaded, they stayed in Essen for a health screening. After he bought the whole lot, he made a selection. In front of the building, there was a courtyard with enough space for them to run. The grooms and assistants stood around my father and the horses ran, kicking up dust. He stood in the middle, snapping his whip.

He focused on what he didn't like and removed the worst horses first.

At first glance he said, "I don't like the feet," or "The hair's not healthy" or "This horse doesn't walk well." He was quick and decisive, and his reviews were brutal.

"This horse is worth nothing. Send him to the abattoir."

When he spotted one he liked, he pointed to it and said, "This one's decent. Send her to a manège." He would then select horses that were good for jumping, and after that, horses that were good for dressage.

He had remarkable intuition. He never wavered from his first judgments. His colleagues used to say that he could *hear* a horse. He listened to a horse run and knew only from the sound it made whether it had irregular steps or some physical problem.

In a group, he found three or four horses that were special. If he said, "This horse will be a champion," he was almost always right. He had an incredible eye. He selected champions and sold them to his friends in the business, of which he had many. He followed those horses for years, as they became what he had thought they would.

At home, my mother and father often had disagreements, but I knew they loved each other. Hedwige and I heard them arguing, and each time we were convinced they were going to divorce. It often happened that, just when we thought there was serious trouble, a few hours later we'd catch them in a long embrace.

To a child, this was very strange behavior.

My mother was elegant, and our father was proud of her beauty and wanted her to be happy. One thing that made her happy was her collection of fur coats. This was a difficult situation to manage, because after World War II my father hated spending money. He never bought anything without haggling, and never paid full price. The irony is that when he was at last satisfied with his negotiating skills and felt it was a bargain he couldn't refuse, he was happy to buy whatever it was.

One day, while walking in town with my mother, she took me into one of her favorite fur shops. At once, she fell in love with an ocelot coat. She adored the fur and caressed the leopard-like spots. It's out of fashion to wear fur now and the ocelot is an endangered animal, but back then an ocelot was coveted.

"What do you think of the coat, Madame Vervoordt?" the dealer asked.

"I like it—can you please deliver it to my home?" she said. "I'll tell you the hour when my husband is there. Don't tell him that I already saw it. If he asks you the price, it's better if you ask for a bit more. Be ready to bargain."

The salesman agreed.

I was shocked by the plan.

I didn't have a chance to say anything before we abruptly left the store.

A few days later, the doorbell rang.

"What a surprise!" my mother said. She opened the door and fresh, cold air entered the house. "Please do come in."

There was the dealer with the coat in hand.

"Thank you Madame Vervoordt. I hope I'm not disturbing the family, but I've got this beautiful coat. I think it might be just the thing for you."

My father sat in his chair, but didn't look up from his reading.

"Oh, I'm so curious.... Shall I try it on?"

The salesman helped her put the coat on. She placed her hand in the pocket and walked back and forth in the sitting room.

She didn't look at my father, until just the right moment.

Without looking at anyone, my father said, "But you don't need another coat."

The salesman said it fit her perfectly. Hedwige and I agreed.

She was beautiful and glamorous. My father tilted his head back. His eyes were bright and fixed upon her. Our eyes were fixed on her, too. There was electricity in the air. My mother smiled. She took the coat off and caressed it. There was a long, silent pause. Then she put it back on again.

"How much?" asked my father.

The negotiations were brief, intense, and successful.

I never told him that I knew about my mother's plan. They were both too pleased with themselves. She got her new coat and he got his deal. Their happiness was hard to deny.

Nuremberg Chest

While I was working in Nadya's shop, my appreciation of art grew every day. One afternoon, I went for the first time to an exhibition and saw the work of Jean Tinguely. One sculpture in particular fascinated me. It was an iron mobile made with simple, everyday objects, but looked so alive. I asked for more information and even dared to inquire about the price. As I recall, it was about 60,000 Belgian francs.[3] As much as I loved the sculpture, I couldn't afford it. Today the work is multiples of what it was then, and it would have been an incredible investment, but I just didn't have the money.

---

[3] At the end of the 1950s, 60,000 Belgian francs (BEF) would be equivalent to 435,000 BEF in 2017 or about $12,850/10,800€.

Later that day, someone told me about an antique chest for sale in a private, first-floor apartment. I went over to have a look. I saw a beautiful sixteenth-century iron chest from Nuremberg. I opened the chest and noticed that the cover was a complex lock. A turn of the key moved a system of eight locks, which opened the lid.

Watching the gears and locks move, I had the same fascination for the old chest that I'd had for Tinguely's work. The chest was like a mobile sculpture made a few hundred years earlier.

Something clicked.

I asked the price. It was one-tenth of the Tinguely.

Without hesitating, I bought the chest.

When it was delivered, I put it in my bedroom. I was always changing my room and swapping objects and furniture. My room was like my private theater. There was a time when I went through a religious phase and I painted my bedroom windows to look like stained glass. I even played a priest and performed mass. My parents and Hedwige heard me reciting verses and chanting in Latin. My family was used to accommodating my whims.

Putting the chest in my room was part of another phase that I've actually never grown out of. My work looking for links between old and new started with the Tinguely and the iron chest. Throughout my life, thousands of objects and works of art have passed through my hands. Over the years, I've learned how to search for the universal, to uncover an essence that is common to both historical and contemporary things. As a reminder, I've kept the chest all my life.

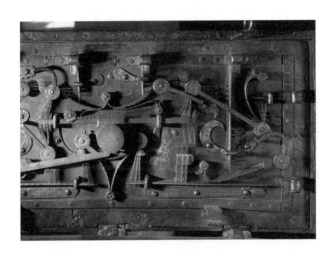

Detail of the complex lock inside the iron chest.

My Father's Terms

In 1961, I was fourteen when I went to England for the first time alone on a buying trip. I had some money because I was already working and had done some business. My parents let me use everything I had earned for the trip. They offered to pay the costs for the travel including the ferry and trains. I could use all of my money for the trade.

My plan was to buy some pieces that I could resell when I returned to Antwerp. I took the boat from Zeebrugge to Ipswich and from there I traveled the rest of the way by train. I stayed with relatives and friends of the family. I went to private sales in great houses in that part of the country. I visited attics full of stuff, and everything I saw was pure discovery.

How did I know what to buy?

It was then as it is now: I bought what I liked.

I bought things that were beautiful and interesting if I could afford them. I followed my intuition. I asked questions and bought things I wanted to know more about. I bought objects that required study, a process that would eventually lead to knowledge.

I was looking for something fresh or new to my eyes and hoping to find something that was undervalued. It must have looked strange that a fourteen-year-old Flemish boy was climbing into attics to look for treasures, but I was thrilled.

When I was a bit older, there was amazing antique silver for sale. I fell for the purity of Huguenot silver and bought as much as possible. Usually people bought silver to put it in a showcase, but I didn't want it behind glass. I wanted to use it.

In my twenties, I made a name for myself by showing people how to live with things. The roots of my discoveries came from hunting around England as a teenager traveling alone.

I returned home from my very first trip with heavy suitcases.

I showed my parents the treasures that I had found. My mother invited her friends for afternoon tea so they could see everything, too.

Within days, everything was sold.

My mother's friends were genuinely enthusiastic. Many of them asked me for more. They wanted to know when I planned my next trip.

This was the start of dozens of trips I took in my youth.

From then onwards, I returned to England during school vacations and whenever I had free time.

At the end of the 1950s and early 1960s, many antiques were coming on the market from the great country houses. It was a trend that had begun earlier in the twentieth century, as the way of life that allowed for the upkeep of such homes changed after World War I. A lot of the big houses were being passed on to the National Trust. Others were demolished or sold, or wings of the houses were sold to save the rest.

The contents of these homes entered the market. For buyers of all ages, it was an incredible opportunity. I came home from trips totally weighed down. I had bags strapped to my back. I stepped off trains and ferries dragging trunks and suitcases along the platform. Sometimes I would carry a table or a couple of chairs in my arms.

I used the profits from each sale to go back to England and hunt for new material. I saved as much as I could to improve my trade. I wanted to have the chance to buy better quality. Sometimes, if I thought something was too expensive, or if I didn't think I had the cash to spare, I called my mother.

She eliminated doubts and encouraged me.

"If you love it, buy it. That's all that matters."

As I took trips to England and built the foundation for my life, I learned about the value of money. I was careful with the profits I earned and tried to save as much as I could.

I developed a method for ordering whenever I went to a restaurant. I looked for the cheapest item on the menu—if I liked it, I ordered it. If I didn't, I looked at the second cheapest item. I continued until I found something that matched my budget and taste. My parents were part of a careful European generation that survived times of war and rebuilt in times of peace. They respected materials.

They never threw food out. I wanted to do the same. My frugal ways were an investment in my business.

It took me a long time to understand how my family's financial situation compared to others. My father bought and sold horses and sometimes land as well. I watched my mother buy old houses and restore them. I didn't realize this was something only people with resources could do. I thought that everyone had the same means we had.

Of course it wasn't true.

We had a good lifestyle. Our parents taught Hedwige and me to treat everything we had with respect. My father liked to be well dressed, and he had a tailor make his suits. When I turned twelve, I was given a made-to-measure suit for my communion. My mother thought it was chic to dress me in a Harris Tweed jacket with knickerbockers and an Eton-striped tie. I thought I looked terrible, because no one else in my class had the same. It was years later when I realized how lucky we were to receive clothes and gifts of handmade quality.

My buying trips continued over the years. But at a certain moment in my teens, I thought there was a chance I could become a horse dealer like my father. His business was strong and the work was exciting. But then one day he said to me, "You're not passionate about horses like I am."

Perhaps it's Freudian, but I struggled against my father. I wanted to do everything differently than he did and maybe that's what he saw. I was discovering my passion, realizing the potential, and setting out to prove it to my family and myself.

The Vervoordt family shares a lifelong passion for horses;
Axel continues the tradition today, riding his horse Raio in the castle's park.

In the end, I see clearly now that I do many things the same way that my father did. It's all in the attitude. However, I didn't understand that when I was young. As a boy, I reacted to my father's toughness with hatred. But it didn't last long. If one of us did something that the other didn't understand, my father made the effort to find a resolution. Moments of silence between us didn't last for hours, but minutes. When I was very young, he would put me on his knees and give me a kiss. As I grew older, it was an embrace or pat on the back. He could be gentle and forgiving. My memories of my father are very black and white—strict toughness on one side and tender affection on the other.

In many ways, we never understood each other. During my late teens, he wanted me to go to university and study economics. I wanted to grow my business. I wanted to continue taking trips to England to buy art, furniture, and antiques. I've always wanted to be an art collector, and for as long as I can remember I've been buying things.

"You have to study and get a job so that you can earn enough money to be a collector if that's what you want," my father said. He didn't realize that was what I was doing all along.

When I was eighteen, I went to a party in London. There was a lot of electricity in the room. Members of the nobility were there, including the daughter of the Duke and Duchess of Bedford. Their Woburn Abbey had opened to the public about ten years before, to help offset heavy taxes and restoration costs. They were selling some possessions and I had the opportunity to buy great pieces like a painting by Pieter Coecke van Aelst.

In order to buy ever better-quality pieces, I needed much more money than I had. Up until then, my budget had come only from the profits from previous sales—there wasn't enough for expensive things.

For the Woburn pieces, I hesitated to ask my father for help, but I had no choice. I told him I needed money. I explained it would take me further than I'd ever been.

"I won't give you the money," he said. "I'll loan it to you."

He explained the terms.

I had to pay the interest on everything I borrowed from him. The interest he charged would be equal to the amount of interest the banks would give if he left the funds in his account. I had to pay him back in installments on the fifteenth of every month. I accepted.

From that day, for the first several years as I built my life, I never had to ask a bank for loans. My father supported me, but he was there, waiting for every cent in return.

If I was on vacation or away from the country on the fifteenth, I paid before I left. I was never allowed to be late. I knew that if I broke the terms he would stop the loans.

For every amount he gave me, he set the same aside for Hedwige. She never asked for it, but he said, "The day she needs her share of the inheritance I have to be able to give it to her immediately."

The first picture I bought from Woburn Abbey is one I have always treasured.

It's a portrait attributed to Thomas Gainsborough of one of the daughters of George III (see page 61). I see this painting every day that I'm home in the castle. It hangs in a private alcove on paneling that came from the Château du Fond l'Évêque in Huy, Belgium. When I think of my father now, I realize that back then he had begun to remove the barriers in my path as I looked to the future. Bit by bit, he built a bridge.

Portrait attributed to Thomas Gainsborough.

Madame Cleiren

In 1965, one of my parents' friends shocked them when she predicted that I would become a dealer.

"How do you know?" asked my father.

"Jos," said Madame Cleiren, calling my father by his first name, "you'll see, because I'll prove it to you."

The Cleiren family had a successful business importing coffee beans and selling to coffee producers in Belgium. Mutual friends introduced us and over time we became close. Madame Cleiren told me that their family had bought a big house.

"There are a lot of display cases in it and I don't have any objects for them. Can you find nice things for us?"

The task was clear.

Madame Cleiren would give me a monthly allowance of about 200,000 Belgian francs[4] and I had to find the best objects I could.

---

[4] 200,000 BEF in 1965 equals about 1,282,000 BEF in 2017 or $38,120/32,000€.

One rule guided whatever I might find: she had to like it. If she didn't like an object, then she wouldn't buy it and I would absorb it into my inventory.

My father couldn't believe that a woman of her stature had so much confidence in me—I was eighteen. It was one thing for him to support me with loans, but it was another thing entirely that someone outside of the family—one of his peers—saw and believed in my potential.

I continued going to England. I was curious, and every discovery encouraged me to learn more about what I had bought. I had more resources to acquire the best-quality pieces. Whenever I met an expert in any field and asked for help I received it. I was surprised by how generous people were with their information. They were so excited that a young person was interested in their work.

They taught me how to look.

They taught me how to examine objects.

They taught me the tricks and secrets of their trade.

A friend of my parents was a diamond dealer with a collection of contemporary art and Daum vases. Once, he unfolded a small blue paper and revealed a pile of diamonds. He handed me a looking glass. He showed me a pure diamond and taught me how to spot a fake.

Another friend of my parents' had a collection of silver, stamps, engravings, and many other things. His door was open to me whenever I had a question. Another friend was a professor and an artist with great knowledge of painting from the Middle Ages. He taught me a lot about different techniques with paint, color, and materials.

Flemish ewer in sculpted wood, first half of the eighteenth century,
sold to the Metropolitan Museum of Art, New York.

Every object I found opened a door to knowledge. I aspired to become a collector, so I kept either the piece that I liked most or the piece that I needed to learn the most about. I would only sell something once I had learned enough about it.

Madame Cleiren's display cases began filling up with objects. One of the discoveries I made was an eighteenth-century decorative Flemish ewer in carved alder wood that now belongs to the Metropolitan Museum of Art in New York.

Later, we expanded the Cleiren collection to include silver. Every now and then, Madame Cleiren allowed me to find a great piece of furniture or a painting.

My love for pottery started then, as Madame Cleiren also liked china and pottery. I found exceptional seventeenth- and eighteenth-century Chinese pieces and early Japanese and Thai monochrome pottery. I bought pieces for my personal collection as well. I learned that she prized quality, and this was a rule I followed for myself.

Madame Cleiren and I worked together for a few years and we remained friends throughout her life. After she passed away, her daughter wanted to keep the serene monochrome china in tribute to her mother. In my mind, this is a symbol of the work that we did together.

Magritte's *La Mémoire*

In the mid to late 1960s, I was working hard and my business was growing. But I decided to follow my father's advice. When I graduated from high school, I went to the University of Antwerp to study economics.

I was bored in class, but I got through it. The content was useful, but I wasn't suited to the pace of life in a classroom. I told my parents that I wanted a change. My father urged me to stay in school.

To give myself time to think, I took a sabbatical year and joined the army to complete Belgium's compulsory military service. The path of a soldier was shorter than the time it took to become an officer, so after boot camp I chose to be a soldier. This gave me the freedom of time. At the end of the required service, I could either continue in the army, return to university, or jump into my business.

In the army, I stated that I would rather avoid conflict. I didn't want to get into a situation in which I'd be asked to shoot anyone, not even an enemy. I got assigned to work in the pharmacy.

Over time, I grew disillusioned with the administrative policies. Every month, my superior ordered an expensive amount of antibiotics and supplies, which we didn't need. They were thrown away at the end of the month.

When I asked him about it, he told me that we had the budget for the supplies, and, if we didn't spend the amount in the budget, then we wouldn't receive it anymore.

"The day we need it," he said, "we won't have the money."

It made sense, but I was disturbed by how much we threw away. I didn't want to sit in the pharmacy with nothing to do. Soon after I started working there, I transformed my space into a cocktail bar. I set up bottles of martini and invited the soldiers to stop by. I served drinks and asked everyone who stopped by a couple of questions:

"Do your parents have anything for sale?"

"Maybe there's something in your grandparents' attic they'd like some cash for?"

It could have been the bar, but the questions caught on.

The guys brought in pictures of things their families wanted to sell. There were great opportunities. I bought many antiques and a bucket full of fantastic eighteenth-century silver. The biggest surprise came when one of my friends walked in and said that his parents had a painting they wanted to sell.

"It's signed by Magritte. Are you interested?"

I was interested, but he didn't have a photograph. We made plans to view the painting and I was fascinated as soon as I saw it.

The title of the painting is *La Mémoire*. It features a woman's head depicted in plaster, resembling a classical sculpture. The head is stained with red blood and placed next to an apple.

The work is part of a series that Magritte returned to over the years, and today it is quite valuable. The family told me the painting was initially sold in an auction during a charity dinner. Someone bought the lot and quickly had buyer's remorse, so they sold it to my army friend's father, who was sitting at the same table.

To make an honest deal, I needed to learn more about René Magritte. I couldn't find many books on the artist, so I asked people I knew for information. Unfortunately, no one had much to offer.

Together with my friend, we went to two salerooms in Antwerp and Brussels to get the painting appraised. We received matching estimates, which quoted the same price for both the low and high amounts. I offered his family a price that was exactly in the middle, which they were happy to accept.

I brought the painting home. My father took one look and said, "How can you pay so much for an ugly painting?"

The price I paid was a lot of money at the time. My father considered the amount equal to a horse or a small house.

Entranced by its magic, I didn't find the painting ugly. I hung it in my room, but the fascination didn't last long. Living with the painting over time, I agreed with my father. It didn't grow on me. No longer seductive or symbolic, the dream-like painting disturbed me. There was too much negative energy.

Whenever I came home from the army, I didn't want to look at it anymore. I turned it around so the front of the picture faced the bedroom wall.

In the back of my mind, I thought about selling the painting. Whenever I got the chance, I asked art dealers I met if they had a Magritte for sale. I wanted to know more about the value of the artist's work. There were several of his paintings for sale at a price much higher than mine—about five times what I had paid. I kept looking for more people interested in Magritte, and eventually I received a different answer. I met some people who didn't have a Magritte to sell, but they wanted to buy one. I mentioned that I'd just heard of several Magritte paintings for sale, and told them the high price. I didn't say that I was willing to sell my Magritte.

Soon after, I was on a break from the army and I took my mother to England on a buying trip. My father called us from Antwerp one evening.

"I've got these crazy people here," he said. "They love your painting and want to buy it."

I didn't know who was going to collapse first.

It turned out that the people who inquired about the Magritte came to our house because they had heard I had one for sale. My father told them he didn't think I was selling my painting, but they insisted.

"He already told us the price."

It wasn't true. I had told them the price of the other Magritte for sale, which I knew from the research. But they'd seen both paintings and fallen in love with mine. They wanted to buy it for the same price.

My father was stunned.

"What should I tell them?"

"Okay," I said, "I'll sell it."

The deal was done—my biggest yet.

My father was happy just to get the painting out of the house.

I returned to the army with new confidence. But I felt guilty. I worried about my friend and his family who originally sold the painting to me. I had paid them about seventy-five times the value of what they had paid at the charity auction. In fact, both of us had sold the work at a price exponentially higher than what we originally paid, but I felt ashamed at the size of my profit.

I told them what happened. I said I regretted that they hadn't made more profit. It might have changed their lives. They said they understood it was the nature of the business; they had done the same thing that I had done. I knew they were honest, because they were always kind to me. Over a period of several years, I paid for the family's holiday trips in honor of their kindness and understanding.

The months of my service stretched on. Before leaving the army, I visited an exhibition at a gallery in Düsseldorf. Walking in, I saw a painting like an old friend. There was "my Magritte" hanging on the wall in a big gold frame. I asked the price. The gallery owner told me the huge sum in deutsche marks—it was already eight times higher than what I had sold it for. I left the gallery and thought that if I was going to become the best dealer that I could be, I couldn't deal in things I didn't know about. I wanted to understand the lessons of art and go deeper into the business. Every discovery needed to be connected to more knowledge.

The Vlaeykensgang
and the Old City

My mother often rode her bicycle to the center of Antwerp to run errands, shop, and see friends. She visited the neighborhoods near Hendrik Conscience Square, where she had bought a few houses. During one of her bike rides she made a discovery that changed my life. I was away in the army when she called.

"Axel, I found something fantastic," she said. "I'm in love and I think you will be, too. It's a small street with several sixteenth-century houses for sale. The whole atmosphere is so serene. Hopefully you can buy a few of the houses."

I went to visit during my next trip home. I walked from the public street through a small door that opened to an almost concealed passage.

It was a place known as the Vlaeykensgang. Linked by a series of narrow medieval alleys, cobblestone paths led to hidden courtyards and what felt like a secret world. Inside, there were a number of fifteenth- and sixteenth-century houses.

I fell in love at first sight.

I learned that many of the houses were built around 1591 and it was the neighborhood where baroque artists Anthony van Dyck and Jacob Jordaens were born. Initially, eleven houses were for sale, and had been on the market for more than a year. My intuition said to act quickly, so I went to discuss the details with the owners, who were two elderly sisters. Even though they lived across town in an adjacent suburb, the sisters told me that they had never visited the Vlaeykensgang after inheriting the houses from their parents years before.

"It's a dangerous part of town," they said. "You should send someone there to collect the rent, but don't go yourself."

In some houses there weren't any tenants at all, because the buildings were in ruins. Yet the sisters wouldn't take a cent less than the asking price. I could either take it or leave it. After reflecting and considering all of my initial hesitations, I followed my intuition and acquired it.

Getting to know the Vlaeykensgang was like stepping inside a novel. The lively neighborhood was full of interesting artists, shops, and dealers. Inside the entrance, the cobblestone alley was bordered on either side by three small houses with windows that faced each other. In a corner there was a communal spout where tenants fetched water. There were a few colorful characters occupying the different houses. There was a woman in her eighties named Rose. Her apartment was immaculate inside and out. She washed her windows twice a day. Every morning, I saw her sweeping the front step and scrubbing it clean with soapy water. She wore a red apron and a crisp white short-sleeve shirt that was tight around her thick arms.

Her next-door neighbor was a woman about the same age who was known to the others as Dirty Louise. Whenever Rose went to fetch water, if she dared to look inside Louise's apartment, Louise ran out of her house screaming at the top of her lungs.

"Don't you dare look inside my windows! Stay out of my business!"

Above Louise, there was a small apartment where a man named Jef lived with his incontinent mother. She wet the bed, and, rather than replacing the mattress, Jef went to the weekly Friday market on a square around the corner and bought a used mattress at auction. He put the "new" mattress on top of the wet one. When I arrived, his mother slept on four mattresses, one piled on top of the next. When she died, he lived alone and didn't have much money. He became known as Jef the Pigeon Thief, because he often went to a public square nearby and caught pigeons to cook at home for dinner.

There were a few other tenants, including an elderly couple. The man was in his nineties. On the first of every month, he knocked on our door with his cane and said it was time to come upstairs to collect the rent. At the end of the 1960s, they paid the equivalent of a little less than ten euros a month for rent and a few cents for water.

I planned to renovate the Vlaeykensgang and use some of the space for my business. I wanted to live in a house and be surrounded by things that I bought and loved. I never wanted a typical shop. I wanted to build my business in a private space where I could invite clients into my world.

I promised not to throw the tenants out. Everyone could stay as long as they liked, and for the next five to ten years many of them did. Some lived in the Vlaeykensgang for the rest of their lives. They watched the spaces transform around them as the restorations uncovered the neighborhood's sixteenth-century character.

The buildings had potential, but the beauty was hard to see. It was going to be a huge job. In the late 1960s, the city considered the area around the Vlaeykensgang to be a slum. Neglected and unloved, some of the derelict buildings had fallen into disrepair. The price I paid was the value of the ground upon which they stood. I wasn't obliged to restore anything. When I went to the city office to register the sale and discuss the plans, I was surprised to be told the area could be torn down. I was given the option to make a housing development with a parking lot on the ground floor.

That wasn't my plan. I wanted to save the old buildings.

I looked for people who shared my passion and wanted to help. I found artists and friends ready to work. I met amateur contractors starting their careers and they joined the project. We cleaned and stripped the crumbling materials. We peeled back the layers. We uncovered beautiful details.

In one room, we found a carved Gothic fireplace. In another, an eighteenth-century marble fireplace mantel. We removed plaster walls and ceilings, and found sculpted sixteenth-century wooden beams with original remnants of polychrome and gold leaf. The back part of the Vlaeykensgang, which was built in the nineteenth

Vlaeykensgang.

century, was a ruin. It was a big contrast with the fifteenth- and sixteenth-century houses, which were still intact because they were built so well.

I needed more help and money than I had. My mother's best friend (one of the women who came to our house every week for afternoon tea) and her husband were well connected with someone in the local government. They suggested I get the Vlaeykensgang classified as a historic property to be eligible for government subsidies. I followed their advice and they arranged a meeting with the minister.

I went to meet him in Brussels. I explained my enthusiasm for the project. I was twenty-two and full of passion. I told him I wanted to save the Vlaeykensgang to restore part of Antwerp's sixteenth-century glory, when the city had become one of the richest cities in Europe.

I thought that, by preserving its historic character, the hidden alleys of the Vlaeykensgang in the dense city center could serve as a space of tranquility. The minister patiently listened to my story.

After the meeting, I dared to ask him out for lunch. He invited his secretary and a woman I assumed was his mistress, as well as a few colleagues, to join us. They chose an expensive restaurant and ordered an absolute feast. He chose the best wine, and bottles kept arriving at the table.

I was too shocked to resist.

At the end of the meal, I received an enormous bill and nearly choked. The minister thanked me with a big handshake.

"I share your enthusiasm," he said. "I'm going to help you save it."

Restored entrance hall of Axel and May's Vlaeykensgang
townhouse, originally built in the early seventeenth century.

A few days later, the bitter aftertaste from the lunch still in my mouth, the minister's wife paid me a surprise visit. I thought it was generous of her to show interest in my work.

She asked to see my stock of furniture and antiques.

She was immediately interested in the best piece of furniture I had—an eighteenth-century English walnut breakfront bookcase. She wrote down the measurements.

I was so happy. I thought if they bought the expensive bookcase, it meant they believed in the project and wanted it to succeed.

A few days later, I received a visitor from the minister's office.

"The bookcase fits perfectly in the minster's house. If you offer it as a present, then they'll classify the Vlaeykensgang."

The words felt like a violation in my body.

I turned the representative away. I transformed my disgust into energy for the big job underway. I understood how easy it was to be taken advantage of. I needed to be more careful.

One five-story building was a big challenge in the project. I added antique wooden floors throughout and transformed huge industrial chimneys, originally used for coffee roasting, into smaller working fireplaces.

I designed an exterior brick tower for a spiral staircase to connect the floors. A classic spiral staircase is built in wood around a central column, but I was highly influenced in the 1970s by the avant-garde Zero movement. I was fascinated by their concept of the void. My dream was to build a staircase without a central column. In its place, I wanted a void—a concept of emptiness.

From the ground up, the spiral concrete staircase would climb five stories with no center core. The job was more challenging

Concrete spiral staircase built
in the Vlaeykensgang in the 1970s.

than anticipated. Before finishing 6 ½ ft. (2 m), the concrete mason who created the cast had a nervous breakdown from the strenuous effort. After a period of rest, he returned to finish the job.

Optical artists like Yaacov Agam inspired me and once the staircase was finished, I wanted to paint the base of each stair using the colors of the rainbow. The rising stairs would subtly change color as the eye adjusted to the moving palette. In the end, the exposed concrete was beautiful as it was, so I decided to forgo the paint.

The stairs were a small element in the project. To complete the rest of the building, the city offered the services of an architect for free. I was grateful for the assistance. The architect worked on the plans and asked several contractors to give estimates for building materials.

Most of the contractors had realistic prices, but they were still too high for my budget. I thought I was saved when one of the architect's friends gave the lowest estimate.

I put my trust in the architect and contractor, but when the work was done the final invoice came. The bill was enormous. It was more than six times higher than the original estimate and they demanded payment. Before the inaugural opening of the complex, I sat on the stairs in the Vlaeykensgang next to my father. I needed so much money. I didn't know if I was going to be able to pay it all back. Tears welled up in my eyes. I'd fallen in love with the Vlaeykensgang and put all of my dreams into restoring its beauty. I was broken by the effort. However, while my mother helped discover it, it was my father who stepped in to save it—he said he would loan me the money. With his help, I vowed to continue.

Love at First Sight

I bought the Vlaeykensgang during Easter 1969. I turned twenty-two that June. I worked day and night in the beginning to renovate the buildings and grow my business to keep everything moving forward. I scheduled time in the mornings for buying. The afternoons were for selling, and I worked on site every evening. I slept very little.

I still liked to go out with friends from time to time. When I did, I had my frugal ways. I hesitated whenever buying an expensive whiskey. I calculated prices in my head to compare the cost of drinks against prices for tiles and wooden beams. Every cent earned could be reinvested into the project.

Around the same time, I had a girlfriend who—I have to be honest—I didn't like that much. Confessions can be harsh when you look back on things. I liked the relationship's atmosphere and the friends we had in common, but her parents thought we had a fixed relationship. They treated me like I was part of the family. I ended the relationship because I was scared.

I justified my decision by saying I didn't want another relationship—at least not before I was thirty. In my mind that's how old my father was when he married. I planned to devote my time and energy to the Vlaeykensgang. The same night, I bumped into my cousin in the center of town. He said he was going to a party at the Rockox House and asked me to come along.

The Rockox House was right around the corner. In the seventeenth century, Nicolaas Rockox was a generous philanthropist, long-serving mayor, collector, and close friend and patron of Flemish artist Peter Paul Rubens. Childless and a widower, he donated his private fortune to benefit the poor. The house where Rockox lived later became a museum.

Newly single, I accepted my cousin's invitation and took a rare night off. When we arrived at the party, I saw a young woman leaning against a pillar on the other side of the room. Time stopped. She had long brown hair and a serene expression. I was fascinated. I couldn't fight the urge to be close to her.

I walked up and offered her a drink. I invited her to dance. She told me that she was eighteen. She was surprised to hear that I was only twenty-two. She thought I was older because I had a mature look.

In the days ahead, we got to know each other and realized it was a small world. May's grandmother knew my grandfather. She said to May: "If Axel is the grandson of Henry Vervoordt then don't get involved. If he's anything like his grandfather, he'll be a real playboy."

Portrait of May Vervoordt on her wedding day, January 5, 1973.

Luckily, May didn't listen and we started dating.

In many ways, it was the best of times and the worst of times. Not long after we met, May's mother was diagnosed with lung cancer. May is the second oldest of six children, and the family didn't even have time to cope with the illness and treatment—two months after the diagnosis, her mother died.

May's older sister went traveling in Japan, and so May cared for her four younger brothers and sisters. She prepared meals for the family and drove her siblings to and from school, while she attended art school herself.

My long days continued. I usually finished work at nine or ten every night. May made dinner for her family and then came to the city with food for me. I didn't have electricity in the unfinished rooms of the sixteenth-century buildings I was restoring. In the middle of the chaos, we dressed a beautiful table with a white linen tablecloth and silver candlesticks and shared a dinner by candlelight.

May drove home alone for a short sleep.

Thinking back, I regret that I didn't drive her home. Our dinners ended at midnight or later, and we were exhausted. There is wonder and magic in building the foundation for your life, but it can be difficult to cope. May's father was a widower with six children. I was deeply sad for their loss. I loved May and her family. But, I struggled.

I thought that if I went to the funeral then I would become part of the family. I wasn't ready for the expectations associated with that responsibility, so I gave them space as they grieved. My mother and Hedwige went to the funeral, but I chose not to. I needed to take some distance to organize my thoughts.

Vervoordt family portrait, circa 1980.
From left to right: Dick, May, Boris, and Axel.

I wanted to marry May, but it was important to make my decision out of total freedom. For our future, I didn't want to say I was pushed into it. I thought that was best for both of us.

Later on, our long days and romantic nights continued. The elderly neighbors like Rose and Louise loved to see May coming and going. They invited her for tea and asked her about her dresses and told her how beautiful she looked.

After May and I knew each other for three years, we broke up.

I thought I needed a free life. But without her, I realized how much I loved her. She's the woman of my life. A few months later, we got back together.

May was twenty-two and I was twenty-five when we married on January 5, 1973.

We lived in the Vlaeykensgang when our son Boris was born in January 1974. Our son Dick was born three years later. May's family started to rebuild as well. After our children were born, May's father remarried.

May has enriched my heart and life. We're partners in spirit and we've made each other stronger. We share the same tastes and often understand each other without words. For many years, May and I have traveled, worked, and lived side by side. We raised our family and built a business together. She's an artist of the ephemeral. With her unique sense for colors and textures, food and flowers, hospitality and the heart of home, she has the magical ability to create an unforgettable feeling in every room she enters.

A Blank Check

I met new clients who were entrepreneurs with a successful road construction business. They were planning to build a new house, and they brought the plans and drawings with them when they came to visit the Vlaeykensgang. In the 1970s, my work selling objects, art, and rare furniture expanded. It was a natural evolution to add interior architecture, because clients liked our home and way of life.

I reviewed the building plans with the clients and offered suggestions. They wanted my advice on how to live in their new home. We toured the studios throughout the Vlaeykensgang where I'd created many different living environments to show my style.

Their project included a large sitting room, and I showed them the rarest furniture pieces I had available. I presented a long list of options so they could take the time to think about what they needed. After the meeting, I invited them to dinner at the Sir Anthony Van Dijck restaurant in the Vlaeykensgang.

"We're happy with the ideas," the husband said during dinner. "I think we'll take everything you proposed."

He handed me a checkbook.

"The problem is," he said, "I don't see very well. So you'll have to write the check yourself. Just fill in the amount you want and I'll sign it."

I stared at the blank check. Was this a test?

I had no experience in situations like this. I wasn't yet thirty years old. I thought about what my father would do. He always said that there's an art to buying and selling. There's an art to making people happy, and, if you're good at it, you can keep clients for life.

From the beginning of my career, I never made up a price in front of the client. It was another piece of advice from my father. Final prices were always calculated in advance. Something I hate as a buyer is the terrible feeling you have when you walk into a shop and notice the shopkeeper looking you up and down. When you ask the price of something, you can sense when they're checking how you're dressed and looking at your car or watch before they calculate the price. I promised I would never do the same.

After dinner, the clients were pleased with their decision. They were one step closer to moving into their house as soon as it was built. I walked away with the blank check and felt honored by the trust. I reviewed the list the following day, and May helped calculate the invoice.

I'll never forget one moment from their first Vlaeykensgang tour. In one room, the wife saw two pairs of silver sauceboats. One pair was eighteenth-century solid silver and the second pair was made with plated silver.

She liked both, but had a question.

"Which pair of sauceboats needs less cleaning?"

The answer was easy.

Antique silver is nearly pure at 92.5 percent. It oxidizes and stains less than plated silver.

"The antique sauceboats are easier to clean," I said. "But they are twenty times more expensive."

"That's okay. We'll take the antique pair," she said. "If they are easier to clean, I'll be much happier."

Turns out that she also understood a lesson in the art of living: be practical.

Lost on the Way
to Glyndebourne

In 1977, May and I were offered tickets to *Don Giovanni* in Glyndebourne. I had recently bought a new Lancia Flavia Pininfarina Coupé, and May and I often drove to England together. As I had done since my youth, I combined travel with opportunities to buy from private collections.

I loved driving along the winding roads in the English countryside. I loved following the curve of a road when its arch was designed to save a single old tree. On the way to Glyndebourne, I must have been distracted by the landscape, because I realized somewhere en route from Kent toward East Sussex that we were desperately lost. We stopped at a little farmhouse for directions. I rang the bell. An old man opened the door. He looked to be in his eighties. He gave me a long look.

"Please come in," he said.

"I'm so sorry, but my wife and I are late for the opera. Can you tell me how to get to Glyndebourne?"

"Please come in. I need to show you something."

I was anxious, but couldn't refuse. I followed him inside.

"This is it."

He handed me a small head made of lacquered wood.

"It looks like you," he said.

I looked at the head in amazement. It was true—there was a slight resemblance.

"Before I die, I want to pass this on to someone," he said. "You're the first person I've met that I think should have it."

I held the head in my hands, and felt like it was my master. I couldn't explain it any other way. I was in love. The coincidences were mysterious and strange. He proposed a price, which I accepted. I paid immediately.

I had hidden pockets made in my jackets and trousers so I could always carry cash. My father told me that if I wanted to buy something, I had to pay at once.

"Once you are serious about doing business, then you have to do it the right way," he said. He was right. I always paid fast, which is why people called me first with new opportunities.

Walking back to the car, I couldn't believe it. I felt drawn to the piece. Back on the road, we arrived too late for the opera and missed the first act. Inside we met George Christie, who invited us over to his house to wait in an astonishing library.

May and I walked into the courtyard and heard the singers rehearsing for the second act. Glyndebourne felt small, private, and absolutely magical in those days.

Axel and the portrait in lacquered wood of the Japanese
Buddhist monk, twelfth to thirteenth century.

Three decades later, the lacquered wooden head is now in the center of the library in the castle. Sometimes I enjoy the process of finding art and objects more than possessing them. But some objects, like this one, have found their place with me. I'm a collector at heart.

I learned from research that the head is a portrait of a Japanese Buddhist monk. It dates to the twelfth to thirteenth centuries. It may be a portrait of Kukai[5]—a scholar, poet, artist, and founder of Shingon Buddhism. Kukai founded a retreat at Mount Koya in Japan. Legend says that Kukai never died—he's in a state of permanent meditation. I think of that when I look at the head. It's a master who offers me guidance. When I'm in doubt about something I look to him for guidance and he helps me find the way. He's strict, but fair. When I'm older, if it feels right, I might offer the head to someone I think should have it, the same way it was offered to me. I hope it will guide whomever it lives with.

---

[5] Also known as Kobo-Daishi

Chaos at Christmastime

My mother was a master at table dressing. One year, around Christmastime, she lit candles and set china, silver, and antique glasses on an old English gateleg table with an interesting patina. It was the first time May was invited to meet my father.

My father had been working in Brussels and he was tired when he returned home. Hedwige and her husband Walter brought their two little sons, Dirk and Christophe. May was nervous and wore a beautiful dress.

My mother served drinks and snacks and then invited everyone to join her at the table. We sat down, and, when Walter pulled his chair close, he bumped the table leg and the whole thing collapsed. My mother screamed.

Glasses slid and shattered.

China crashed to the floor.

Silver clanked to the ground.

Vases and flowers toppled over.

Hedwige ran into the kitchen and burst into tears. A few minutes later, my mother joined her. "It's so terrible," she cried.

Walter apologized, but it wasn't his fault. My father stayed calm and nearly silent. May offered to help clean up, but my father wouldn't accept it. He put his hand on her shoulder.

"Come child," he said. "Let's have a chat on the sofa."

My father had a generosity of spirit in moments like this. He had a wonderful sense of humor, and I understand why he had great friends. He was considerate, and could be lavish with attention.

At home, he wanted to have the best food possible. When eating meat, he ate everything. If you didn't eat the fat, he said, "You didn't know the war. People were fighting over a piece of fat."

That night, dinner was ruined before our eyes, but he made May feel welcome. The next day, he pulled me aside.

"Axel, she's nice and I like her very much. Don't let her get away."

And then, a horseman at heart, he said, "I have one more thing to say: she has really nice legs."

The memory is a fine one, but I can't shake the feeling that my father wasn't feeling well that night. It was the start of a period leading up to his death when he often felt tired and sick. I regret that May didn't meet him earlier, in his grand moments. He commanded horses and teams of people. He had big days.

Another Man's Treasure

I feel a duty to old buildings to be their guardian. When I restored one of the Vlaeykensgang's main houses, which is now the Sir Anthony Van Dijck restaurant, there was a small passage that needed windows. When restoring something, you look for answers and, if you allow it, the search leads you to unexpected places.

One afternoon I was walking in the center of town when I saw a dumpster on the side of a street. Mixed with the trash, I saw window frames. The glass was still intact. The sixteenth-century oak frames and ironwork for the hinges were original. I couldn't believe it. I ran for help and went back to the dumpster to retrieve them. We delivered the windows to the site and they were the same size, down to the centimeter, that I needed.

The sixteenth-century windows are still in place decades later. They look like they've always been there. Today, no one would believe that part of the Vlaeykensgang was a ruin and the windows came from a dumpster next to a demolished building.

Before we moved to the castle, someone took a photo of Boris and Dick sitting together next to the same windows during a party. Looking at the photo, I'm reminded of how full life can be when you live surrounded by history.

Dick and Boris in the Vlaeykensgang in front
of the sixteenth-century windows recovered nearby.

The Biennale des Antiquaires

I was thirty-five when I participated for the first time in the Biennale des Antiquaires at the Grand Palais in Paris in September 1982. My friend Didier Aaron encouraged me to exhibit and helped me procure an invitation. The Biennale had been a can't-miss event for the *beau monde* for decades. My taste was relatively unknown outside of Belgium, and participation offered a platform to share my work with new audiences.

It takes considerable time and effort to prepare for the Biennale. In some ways, you could say that I had been preparing for it my whole life. From dozens of buying trips, I had many great things to show, like royal gilt silver, exceptional furniture, and grand mirrors. By that age, my passion for Asian objects was growing stronger. A Chinese collector I had recently met offered me pieces from his collection, including sixteenth-century Japanese folding screens and ancient pottery. I also had a rare Gothic oak table, which looked primitive and architectural. It had been published in a book on world furniture. I had an extraordinary, ornate rococo corner cupboard with detailed carvings and original paint—it was pure fantasy. I had a superb Antwerp cabinet with tortoiseshell and carved boxwood figures. Each piece was unique, and yet one might say they were things that didn't traditionally go well together. But I saw a common thread of beauty connecting all of the pieces. For the stand, I imagined creating a space in which every corner had a different style. The challenge was to bring harmony to it all.

I arrived at the Grand Palais and stood underneath the iron, steel, and glass-vaulted roof. I was surprised to have received a large stand near the entrance, which included parts of the staircase. At first, I made a tour to see the other exhibitors. In every stand, I saw workers building elaborate wooden constructions, erecting walls, and carving out niches.

My heart sank.

I had prepared a concept in my mind, but had done little else. I had great objects, but I brought almost nothing else with me. I had no plans to build anything. I started to second-guess myself. I thought I was too young to be at such a prestigious event and no one would understand what I was doing. I was sure that the exhibitors and public would think that I was just a country boy who was in over his head. I was headed for disaster and convinced I wouldn't be invited back to participate for a second time.

Weeks of work and preparation caught up with me. I felt a weight on my shoulders. I walked through the Grand Palais and

Holy Roman Emperor Ferdinand II of Austria
and Princess Eleonora Gonzaga of Mantua.
Rare Italian *pietra dura* cabinet, seventeenth century.

headed for the exit, planning to take a short walk to get some fresh air. When I got outside, I took a few steps into the grass and couldn't go any further.

I lay down on my back and looked up. The September sun was hot and high in the sky. I closed my eyes and fell into a deep sleep.

I woke up a few hours later. No one had disturbed me. I felt refreshed, but I couldn't shake the heavy thoughts. Uncertain of what to do, I walked back inside and saw the other stands with fresh eyes. The workers had made progress, but everything that I thought would become beautiful had taken a turn in the other direction. The wooden interiors and intricate niches were covered with fake marble, animal prints, and faux paneling. What had looked so inspiring at the start was now unrecognizable.

I had an epiphany.

I didn't want any construction or decoration at all. The only preparation I would do was elimination. In the stand, I removed the carpet to reveal the concrete floor. I took away the ceiling, so that the structural beams of the Grand Palais stayed visible above. Rather than building a stand outward, I peeled mine back to the essentials. I did the same with the art. I placed everything I brought with me, exactly as it was. Real is stronger than fake. The quality of each piece spoke for itself.

I didn't even know the word "loft" yet, but that's what my first stand in Paris became. It was a raw, industrial space with high ceilings, bare concrete floor, great furniture and art. I placed all of the royal silver in the center of the stand on a table covered with a worn, seventeenth-century point de Lucca tablecloth. Above the table, I hung a rock crystal chandelier very low. I placed Japanese

European and English silver, seventeenth and eighteenth century,
on a rococo Bavarian china cupboard, eighteenth century,
presented on the stand at the Biennale des Antiquaires in 1982.

screens alongside the Gothic table. I threw several eighteenth-century silk carpets on the stairs and installed a cabinet, inspired by how I imagined the setting in which Louis XIV had received Suleiman Aga, presuming the latter to be the ambassador of Ottoman Empire sultan Mehmed IV. On the upper part of the stand, there were great silver-gilt tankards, which were like an abundance of riches. There were ornate, seventeenth-century Córdoba leather walls.

When I finished, I took a step back.

Everything was exposed in a casual way and it was eclectic. It was my view of how a rich artist might live. I thought to myself, "If nobody else likes it, that's okay, because I like it." I was prepared to accept whatever happened.

I didn't have to wait long to find out.

The fair opened and we were swarmed with visitors. I met Valentino, Hubert de Givenchy, the Rothschild family, Rudolf Nureyev, and Yves Saint Laurent and Pierre Bergé, who all became clients and friends. People fought for the embroidered tablecloth and, in the end, a friend of Givenchy bought it. Ralph Lauren acquired the Gothic table.

I met pianists Marielle and Katia Labèque together with musician John McLaughlin, and we became friends for life. John and Katia were living together in Monte Carlo and, shortly thereafter, I started working on their apartment.

I met Betty Gertz's assistant, who called Betty to say, "This is the guy we need to design your home in Dallas."

Betty came to visit me in Belgium later that year and we have been friends ever since.

The first piece I sold from the stand was the pair of sixteenth-century Japanese screens through a prominent dealer. I was honored that they had been sold through a well-respected dealer who was also featuring screens at her stand. It boosted my confidence. At the end of the fair, the dealer returned and told me her client had backed out. I was disappointed because many people had made offers throughout the Biennale, but I had proudly told them the screens had already been sold. Many years later, I saw the dealer again and asked what had happened. She said, "Axel, the best favor I ever did for you was to block the sale of those screens, because the price you were asking was much too cheap."

I was disappointed at the time, but I'm happy to say that I still have the screens and have experienced great joy from living with them over the years.

Throughout the Biennale, we had many visitors who told me that the stand was a revelation in style. The reaction was surprising and the success was immense. It changed the trajectory of my life. To have the chance to share my work at an international fair was exciting and humbling. I made friends who have added new dimensions to my life. I think few of them would have believed that, before the opening, they could have found me in front of the Grand Palais sleeping in the grass.

But It Ain't a Bugatti

In a sale in the 1980s, I saw a Rembrandt Bugatti sculpture of a walking leopard. I was struck by the depiction of the animal's physical strength and power and amazed at how Bugatti captured the leopard's distinct movement in a stationary bronze figure. I loved how all of the energy passed from the body through the curved tail and connected to the earth.

Bugatti had a connection to Antwerp—his favorite place to study was the Antwerp Zoo—but his work wasn't my specialty. Yet, whether the bronze was contemporary, modern, or historical wouldn't have changed the connection to it that I felt. The leopard was timeless. We researched the object and discovered that it was a cast made by A. A. Hébrard during Bugatti's lifetime. I bought it and decided to exhibit it in my stand during the next Biennale des Antiquaires.

In the stand, the leopard caught the eye of one of my best friends. She had never heard of Bugatti, but was drawn to the bronze's energy. She asked how much it cost and, when I told her the price in francs, she said that it was expensive, but would come back later with her husband so that he could see it. She and her husband shared an eye for quality and they always agreed together on which works to add to their collection.

They returned a couple of hours later.

There was just one problem.

She thought I had quoted the price in Belgian francs, rather than what I actually said in French francs, which was about six times higher. We corrected the misinterpretation and calculated the conversion.

"Oh, it's even more expensive than we thought," she said.

But they had fallen in love. They wanted to live with the Bugatti.

Later on, I took them for lunch at La Stresa and what happened there had us rolling with laughter. As we sat at the table enjoying a great bottle of wine, my friend looked around the restaurant. On a top shelf along one of the walls, she saw a sculpture of a panther.

The next time the waiter passed our table, she pulled him aside.

"Sir, what a coincidence. That's a nice bronze panther you've got there."

"Yes madam," he said, "But it ain't a Bugatti."

Walking Leopard, bronze sculpture by Rembrandt Bugatti.

The Ming Porcelain Cargo

In early 1984, Betty Gertz called from Dallas to say that she was coming to Europe with her friend David Howard. There was an upcoming sale at Christie's in Amsterdam, and she asked if I would like to go with her. She said that a cargo ship full of seventeenth-century late Ming porcelain had been recovered from a shipwreck in the South China Sea and Christie's was selling the collection at auction. I was pleased with her invitation, but I didn't know much about the sale. My first feeling was that I'm not very keen on blue-and-white china. I hesitated, but, to please Betty, I agreed to go. We arrived in Amsterdam, and, once we walked inside Christie's, I was astonished. I'd never seen anything like it.

Recovered in the early 1980s from a shipwreck dating back to the mid 1600s by British explorer Captain Michael Hatcher, the cargo included bowls, dishes, vases, vessels, cups, jars, and more.

There were thousands of pieces. I couldn't find two that were identical. I looked at as many objects as I could, and each piece had a unique design that looked like action painting. The Hatcher cargo changed my perception of what Ming porcelain could be. The painting was so free and expressive that it seemed modern. Circles, details, and flourishes had individual character. Even in the smallest details, I saw the freedom of the artisan's hand. Betty and I were in awe.

There were many critics at the time, however. Other dealers and colleagues said that the market wasn't ready for this amount of Ming porcelain. Because the pieces had been submerged in saltwater for over three hundred years, the original shiny glaze was gone, leaving a matte surface. The once bright blue-and-white colors were now soft and faded. Yet, that's exactly what I loved. I prefer matte over shiny. Made with kaolin and then fired, these pieces were completed by the sea. Nature gave the original work an extra dimension. I was thrilled that, upon the recovery of the shipwreck, each piece could find a new home.

After the viewing, I worked quickly to arrange for art historians from my team to inspect the pieces one by one. It was an enormous job. There were individual lots that included a single piece, and then there were lots consisting of two pieces, three pieces, five pieces, and bigger lots that included dozens or even one hundred pieces. Overall, there were thousands in total. The inspection was necessary.

I wanted to know how to determine the quality of each lot. I wanted to know in which of the group lots there were, for example, three exceptional pieces combined with several of lesser quality.

Art historians from the Axel Vervoordt Company
review the individual pieces of Ming porcelain from the Hatcher cargo.

Or whether one lot included all amazing pieces or whether they were all poor. The team worked hard to put together reports on as many of the pieces as possible. I felt confident in the days and hours leading up to the sales—the first was held in March 1984 and the second was in June.

May and I went with Betty and David. There was a lot of publicity in Amsterdam, and around the industry in general, which contributed to a high level of excitement and anticipation.

The first lots were announced and the sale started.

I thought, "If I'm going to do this, I'm going to go big."

With my research in hand, I started buying. And buying. And buying.

Betty and I had made a deal.

She bid on the even lot numbers and I bid on the odd lots. And if she didn't want the even lot, then I bought it, too.

Betty was laughing, and, the more lots we won, the more fun we had.

There were so many lots that the auction lasted for hours. May had joined us at the start, but she left Christie's and went to the Van Gogh Museum and Rijksmuseum. She returned in the evening when all of the museums were closed.

I was still bidding.

She thought I was completely crazy to buy that much china. When she saw me, I had a cramp in my right arm, so I used my left arm to prop it up so I could keep bidding.

In the end, Betty and I bought the majority of what was for sale. I bought over 7,500 pieces. We filled vans and brought the pieces to Belgium, though not for long.

Blue-and-white Ming porcelain, circa 1640, from the Hatcher cargo,
displayed in the castle's dining room.

Shortly after, I participated in the China Fair in London and displayed the porcelain to great success, selling pieces to museums and collectors.

In September 1984, I participated for the second time in the Biennale des Antiquaires in Paris. I had requested a bigger stand, but unfortunately couldn't get one. Behind a wall at the back of the stand, there was a large room with a very high ceiling. I asked if we could use this space to display the blue-and-white porcelain.

I wanted to make a statement.

Thankfully, the organizers agreed.

To build the stand in less than three days, our team worked a full day and night, and then the following day without sleep. We made a 23-ft.- (7-m-) high buffet that looked like a tower. We hung strings from the ceiling to create perspective and exact proportions just like they did during the Renaissance. We built every shelf according to the ratio of the golden section and worked tirelessly to get it right.

We tested the result by placing some of the porcelain in position. Even smaller vases on the top shelves looked impressive due to the perspective of the big buffet. Every angle gave a dramatic view. We installed a selection and waited for the visitors to arrive.

Within minutes, it caused a sensation.

People queued inside and outside the stand.

To protect the fragile pieces, we added a rope to keep guests from crowding in too close, and led people through in small groups. We had visits from French actors, politicians, royals, and members of famous families from America, Europe, and the Middle East. The response was tremendous. Some clients returned multiple times and brought their sons and daughters to choose more. Those that bought also wanted to take their porcelain home with them, so more of our staff came from Antwerp just to help pack.

Betty's collection set off her own sensation in Dallas. It was a fortuitous investment for both of us. Early the following year, in 1985, Captain Hatcher's private collection was auctioned at Christie's. The final prices for his pieces were high, multiples of what we asked for them, so I wasn't able to buy anything. However, I was happy that my clients could be pleased with their purchases and have confidence in the market.

Thirty years later, May and I keep the same, original selection of our blue-and-white porcelain in the castle's dining room. I love the palette of blue and white in a dining room, because any change in color comes from the food and people who come together there. A few years ago, I returned to Dallas to work with Betty again. In her new home, I designed white, carved wooden brackets to display her collection of Hatcher porcelain as a reminder of a festive way of life.

The Castle of 's-Gravenwezel

From the beginning of our relationship, even before we were married, May and I shared a little farmhouse with Hedwige and Walter in the Belgian polders near Lapscheure, just outside of the coastal town of Knokke. The views of the flat landscape around the farm were peaceful and relaxing.

We traveled to the countryside as often as we could. May and I worked on Saturdays and so our weekends were limited to Sundays. We returned to Antwerp early Monday morning to start a new week. After Boris and Dick were born, we had a lot to pack for only one night, but it was worth the effort. Hedwige and Walter also had two sons and, when we started to outgrow the little farmhouse, we wanted to look for something bigger.

One Sunday afternoon, Hedwige and I were touring the narrow, winding roads near our house when I spotted a charming farm near the village of Moerkerke. I stopped the car and walked toward the front door of the house. I saw people in the yard and asked them if there were any farmhouses like this one for sale in the area.

"How'd you know?" a man answered. "We just decided to sell this house today."

We couldn't believe our luck.

He offered us a tour and it was exactly what we were looking for. When Hedwige asked about the price, it was nearly half of what we thought he might say. We didn't dare to say yes immediately, although we didn't think about it for long.

We bought it later the same day.

As time passed, we enjoyed the house immensely, alternating visits with Hedwige's family. I've always loved nature and gardens and I loved to be in the country. As my business expanded into architecture and interior design, I had met the landscape architect Elisabeth de Lestrieux and we started working together designing houses and gardens. I was inspired by her horticultural knowledge and ability to plant based on color and scent. I fell in love with single-colored gardens like the White Garden at Sissinghurst Castle in Kent. I dreamed of creating a series of single-colored gardens of my own.

As the business grew, the hour drive from Antwerp to our farmhouse seemed longer than it was. Time was precious. May and I wanted a weekend retreat that was only fifteen or twenty minutes from the Vlaeykensgang. I mentioned the idea to a friend who had a chateau near the village of Schoten outside of Antwerp. On the property, there was a ruin in need of restoration. It was an

The castle of 's-Gravenwezel.

old orangery, and I thought I could transform it into something magical.

Unfortunately, the owner didn't want to sell. But he said that we could rent the orangery for a reasonable price in exchange for restoration. I agreed, and we worked hard to rebuild the orangery and surrounding gardens into our weekend home, investing a lot of time and effort.

We went more and more often to the property, even departing from Antwerp in the middle of the week and commuting back to the city for work and school until the weekend.

The boys were happy to be surrounded by nature. Behind the orangery there was a forest and a shallow moat that wound its way around the border of the property. One day, Boris went for a walk and cut tree trunks and collected pieces of wood to build a bridge to cross the moat. When he showed the bridge to me, I was so proud—it was a work of art. He had made a real bridge with details that included a small handrail. I asked the chateau's owner to come and have a look.

"Isn't it amazing?" I said.

He took a look at it.

He pulled his leg back, and, with one swift kick, he smashed Boris's bridge, sending wood flying in every direction.

"You can't make anything here," he said, waving his arm. "You've only hired that piece of land and can't go any further."

My anger burned like a blue flame ready to explode.

I took Boris back inside the house. I told May that we wouldn't rent another house again. I didn't want to follow a landlord's rules and risk the cruelty he had showed my son. I made plans to leave.

I told May's father the story of what happened. He knew a lot about the local real estate market and I asked him to keep his eye out for interesting properties. I wanted to have a plot of land with a small house that we could use for the weekends, with enough space for horse riding and planting gardens.

He asked around and, not long after, he told me that there was a castle in 's-Gravenwezel for sale, which wasn't far from Antwerp. The property included a large piece of land.

It sounded nice, but I wasn't interested. I didn't even want to have a look. We were searching for a weekend country house, not a castle. I thought the Vlaeykensgang was beautiful, and it would be folly to leave what we had created to move to a castle.

We continued living in Antwerp and spent weekends in the orangery. Part of our weekly Sunday brunch tradition included a short drive to the local bakery. Dick and Boris loved to come along and ride in the back of our Mitsubishi SUV. One Sunday morning, I asked Boris and Dick to tidy their rooms. I felt like going to the bakery alone. Instead of driving the usual route, without really knowing the way, I drove in the direction of the castle. Before I had the chance to find it, I had a change of heart.

I didn't want to see it and risk falling in love.

I felt that I would be betraying the Vlaeykensgang, which I didn't want to leave. I changed my mind.

Without looking, I spun the steering wheel suddenly to turn back.

There was a huge crash.

When I opened my eyes, I was lying in a ditch.

I climbed out of the car and stood up. I was disoriented. I didn't know what had happened. I was in shock, but didn't feel any pain. My car had flipped over and was completely totaled. I hadn't been wearing a seatbelt. I looked to the street and realized that another car had crashed into mine.

I went to check on the other driver. A few police officers and an ambulance arrived to help the injured. They towed the cars away, and offered me a ride home.

May saw the police car pull in the driveway and came rushing out of the house. I told her the truth. I said that instead of going to the bakery, I had been driving to see the castle her father had told us about when I caused a major accident. We both clutched our hearts, thankful that Dick and Boris hadn't been in the car.

The rest of the day, as the shock subsided, I couldn't stop thinking about the accident and the castle.

"May, I have no injuries," I said. "I think we should try again."

I convinced her and we tried again.

When we arrived at the castle, a gardener named Albert opened the wooden entrance gate and said that he had been feeding the sheep.

"We've heard the castle is for sale and wanted to have a look."

"I'm sorry, but it's sold," he said.

I couldn't believe it—we were too late.

Albert told us that, a few days earlier, a couple from Holland had visited and immediately took a two-month option to buy while the details were being worked out.

Even though another couple had taken an option to buy, Albert allowed us to tour the property. We walked with him over a cobblestone bridge that crossed a moat and stood in front of the castle in a big, open courtyard overlooking a huge park.

First picnic in the castle's park.
From left to right: Boris, May, Dick, Mani, and Axel.

During our visit of the grounds, he opened one of the property's iron gates. I couldn't believe my eyes when I took a closer look and saw the date 1747 with the initials AV carved in the center—I was born in 1947. My initials are AV.

We continued and saw a second iron entrance gate carved with the initials MSAV—May's maiden name is Schelkens, and these were our initials when we met. May and I looked at each other—we were in love with the place.

Nearly all of the important decisions I've made in my life happened without hesitation—I acted in seconds. When I saw May, I knew that I had to talk to her. When I saw the Vlaeykensgang, my intuition told me to acquire it quickly. Walking through the gates of the castle, I felt that I had come home.

In truth, it wasn't the first castle that we had visited with the idea that we might buy it. A few years before, one of my parents' friends—who had given me a lot of advice about art over the years—suggested that I buy a chateau. He even showed me a moated, medieval castle that was for sale. May and I went to have a look, but its surroundings were not ideal. The house had very little light inside.

Seeing the castle of 's-Gravenwezel for the first time was a different experience. It's also a moated, medieval castle that was first mentioned in historical documents in the year 1108. The castle hadn't been sold since 1729.

Between 1730 and 1780, however, a big transformation was made to create a grand atmosphere, a *château de plaisance*. Large windows were added on the south façade, which contrast with the smaller medieval windows on the north and east façades. The eighteenth-century windows gave the house so much light, and, although I didn't like the castle's interior when I first saw it, the 172 acres (70 hectares) of land with gardens, outbuildings, and a park were breathtaking.

It was a dream come true.

We thanked the gardener and walked back over the bridge.

"Before we go," I said. "There's one more thing I want to ask you."

I said that I was interested to meet with the current owners and asked if he could arrange it. He said that he would try. I was surprised to receive confirmation that a few days later, on Wednesday afternoon of the same week, I could meet with the family's representatives.

I looked forward to the appointment all week.

A couple of hours before the meeting was scheduled, I was in my office in the Vlaeykensgang when the doorbell rang. I opened and met a Dutch couple who told me they had recently bought a few apartments in a nearby suburb. They wanted to combine them into a single home and asked if I could help design and furnish it. Through our introductions and a brief conversation that followed, I realized that this was exactly the same couple who had placed an option to buy the castle of 's-Gravenwezel.

"But, if I'm not mistaken," I said, "haven't you bought an historic property nearby?"

They said yes.

But after a family discussion, their children warned them against buying a big castle. They loved to travel, and the children said it would be more convenient and involve less maintenance to live in an apartment building.

I was astonished by the news. The castle was available.

I arrived at the meeting with the notary of the family that was selling the castle and said that I was ready to buy.

"But the castle's already sold," he said.

"I've heard differently."

He asked for an explanation. I said that, by pure coincidence, I met the buyers when they asked me to work on their new apartment.

The notary said that, even if what I said was true, nothing could be done until the two-month option expired—at 4 p.m. on August 17.

After the meeting, I contacted our lawyer for advice.

We knew it was a difficult situation.

One nephew of the family, whom I knew well, had initially inherited the castle, but, after a family dispute, he renounced his inheritance, and the group of heirs now included forty-two family members. Getting them all to agree once again on a second offer would be a challenge.

We also knew that we had to take action as soon as the option expired.

I asked the notary if it was still possible to buy property as it was done in the old days, with a firm handshake. I had grown up learning about my father's business ethics. Once he agreed to buy a horse, it was his horse. Even if the horse had an accident, got sick, or dropped dead, he paid what was owed. My father always said, "My word is my word."

The notary said that a handshake was still valid as long as there were witnesses. I made my intentions known and planned to buy the castle the second the option expired.

Wisteria in bloom in the castle's walled garden.

I invited the original heir to a get-together with our company's staff and a few close friends. Betty was in Belgium to work with us on her Dallas house, so she came along and brought a jeroboam of champagne to celebrate.

We met in the courtyard in front of the castle on the afternoon of August 17, 1984. My eyes were fixed on the notary's watch.

The hands struck four.

"Is everybody watching?"

I grabbed the heir's hand and clasped it together with mine.

"I'm buying the castle!"

Everyone erupted in applause.

The notary made a record of a few of the eyewitnesses and asked them to sign, while we poured champagne. The castle of 's-Gravenwezel was going to be our new home.

Ghost Stories

May and I returned home to the Vlaeykensgang on the day we bought the castle, and Marc Paesbrugge, the chef of the Sir Anthony Van Dijck restaurant, came to speak to us. He said that his restaurant had been awarded two stars and was becoming a success. He needed a bigger space, and if he found one, he would have to leave.

The timing was fortuitous. As we had our plans to move, Marc could take over the much larger spaces we were using for our home, to which he agreed. Shortly after, the press announced the restaurant would change locations two years later, in 1986. The castle's renovations would have to be complete by then. I wasn't sure we would have enough time.

The first Sunday that we owned the property, I invited a few friends from Ghent to the castle to take a look. They asked if it was possible to bring another friend with them, a professor and writer named Bernard Lietaer. I gave Bernard a tour of the castle and he saw sacred details that I could not. He taught me about the study of proportions and the golden section. Jef Verheyen first introduced me to the concepts years before. Bernard helped deepen my understanding by showing me how those concepts related to the castle. The lessons he taught me that day and during the days that followed were important in restoring the castle, understanding its history, and learning how to live in it. With Bernard's help, as well as assistance from art historians and our own research, we saw what parts of the castle were original and what was added at a later date.

The original owners kept some of the historical documents for themselves, but I was grateful to acquire the original garden and park plans. There are 172 acres (70 hectares) of land surrounding the castle, and my dream of space for horse riding and single-colored gardens could become a reality. We started the renovations during Easter 1985.

Every morning, I went to the castle to give the workmen their daily instructions. During the day, I worked at the office and returned to the castle each evening to check on the day's progress. During any free time, I sat in one of the towers of the castle, in a room that I now use for concentration and to feel the energy of the building. I studied the architectural plans and read books about proportions, architecture, and esoteric knowledge. My way of restoring is to understand that history is the leader and my duty is to follow. I had a lot to learn.

The more time I spent at the castle, the less time I spent in the Vlaeykensgang. The energy shifted.

A series of strange things happened that were never explained.

While we still lived in the Vlaeykensgang, and following a day of open house, someone broke into our private bathroom and stole a pair of May's Bulgari earrings that I'd recently given to her. We were in shock. The same evening that the earrings were stolen, we found May's antique pearl and diamond choker on the floor. It was shattered to pieces—a deliberate act. We were afraid and never found out who was responsible.

The next day, I was sitting with my mother in my office after a long day of work. It was dark out. I went to close a heavy iron gate that was an entrance door that we locked every night before we slept. I had just walked back into the office when we heard a loud crash.

We ran to the doorway.

The gate I had just closed was wide open.

Appearing out of nowhere, we saw a figure of white light, rolling like a cloud of smoke. It moved fast and disappeared into a porphyry vase.

We were too terrified to speak.

We didn't waste time speculating—it was time to go.

The next day, several moving vans arrived to transport some furniture, including a beautiful marble table inlaid with circular designs that were symbols of friendship. As the vans drove away, a rope that was used to secure the table came loose and the table fell, crashing on its side. The marble broke into a thousand pieces.

I was emotional about leaving the Vlaeykensgang. For more than seventeen years, May and I had lived and worked in the sixteenth-century buildings. It was where we started our life together, built the business, and raised our young boys. I knew the cobblestone paths, the attics, cellars, hidden courtyards, and every square inch of each house. I spent hours restoring every room. We love it so much that we never wanted to sell it and we never have.

Despite the charm of living in the center of town, the neighborhood is densely built and the close proximity of the houses filters the direct sunlight. Moving to the castle meant having more space. We would be surrounded by nature. We would have big windows that would let the light in.

I knew that I would never possess the castle; its history stretches back almost one thousand years. I'm the happy caretaker—a custodian for the present. I studied its history to restore it with respect, but I know that I'm the temporary owner. In the beginning, I felt called to the Vlaeykensgang. I felt called to do the work that the castle needed, and still feel that this work continues today. I'm constantly learning. History is full of lessons, even if it works in mysterious ways.

Rudolf Nureyev
and October Snow

The beauty of life happens in unexpected moments.

I met Rudolf Nureyev for the first time in Paris during the Biennale des Antiquaires in September 1982. He bought the Córdoba leather for the walls in his New York apartment in the Dakota, where we later stayed as his guests. He had fantastic style—eclectic, full, and warm.

May and I loved to attend his performances as often as we could. His charisma, talent, and beauty are well known. He was ballet's superstar and the rare type of artist that makes you wonder if there will ever be anyone like him again.

I'll always remember the big audiences he attracted whenever we saw him. The moment he appeared on stage, their enthusiasm was electric. When he jumped into the air he could stay there like a hovering angel, as though time stood still.

In our private moments together, I remember Rudi as quiet, sensitive, and mysterious. After we bought the castle in August 1984, he had a few performances in Belgium in October. As usual when he was in town, May and I organized an intimate dinner for him in the Vlaeykensgang.

Sometimes he'd bring a friend or another person, but I remember that he often came alone. He never wanted too many guests. He wore a big shawl and a casket hat. He loved old, worn-out glamour—used silver and aged gold reflected by candlelight. He loved sumptuous food presented as in a still-life painting, and wine served in antique glasses or gilded beakers. That was the way May and I loved to receive guests in those days. It was the way we lived. He took his time to visit our home and walked slowly and silently through each room, as though he were breathing in the atmosphere.

During dinner, we told Rudi we were moving twenty minutes outside of Antwerp. We had already packed some things to move from the city to the country. From the beginning, we wanted to spend every weekend at the castle as a family, to get to know the house and its environment. We temporarily furnished some of the rooms to get a feeling for each space. It gave us time to think about how we would live there after the restorations were finished. I needed time to study the volumes in each room and understand their purpose in order to create my vision for the castle. There's an art to occupying a house. The atmosphere should reflect your personality, character, and emotions. Above all, it should make you happy. This process takes time.

Following our dinner, Rudi's secretary phoned unexpectedly the next day. "Mr. Nureyev would love to see the castle."

Winter view of the park from the castle's terrace.

There are some requests that you cannot refuse.

We immediately started preparing for his visit later that evening. It was pure improvisation.

We took boxes and stacked them one on top of the other in a central room that luckily already had a working fireplace. This room is now our library, but we didn't know that at the time. I quickly furnished the space in a way that was inspired by Zeffirelli's film *La Traviata*.

I had a beautiful Napoleon III needlework carpet, which was the same size as the space. We placed textiles, carpets, shawls, sheets, and everything we had on top of the boxes. May arranged flowers and dozens of candles throughout the rest of the many unfurnished rooms.

That evening, if my memory is correct, Rudi was performing at the Forest National theater in Brussels. Although May and I were busy, we went to see the production. After it ended, we waited for him outside.

When he arrived, he said that he didn't want to go with his driver and preferred to ride in our car. I had recently replaced a bigger car with a smaller BMW. I told him the drive from Brussels to the castle would take about an hour. He asked if he could sit in the backseat and rest.

Before we got on the highway, he stretched his legs out, in between the two front seats. He put his feet on top of the gearshift between May and me and fell asleep.

I didn't know what to do. If I asked him to move his feet he would wake up. If I moved the gearshift, he would wake up. He was exhausted, so I didn't do anything.

The illuminated castle reflected in the moat.

I drove the forty some miles (70 km) home in second gear, while Rudi slept in the backseat. Cars raced past us on the highway. We were anxious to get home to spend the night in our new castle, and the slow drive seemed endless.

In the north of Belgium where we live, we don't have much snow in winter. When it does snow, it usually doesn't accumulate and never stays for very long. It is almost unheard of to have snow in October.

I remember that it snowed that night.

Arriving via the long, narrow cobblestone driveway leading to the entrance gates, Rudi woke up.

The ground all around us was white, full of a light dusting of fresh snow. The falling flakes created a hazy fog, lit by the car's headlights as we approached. Without being asked, our concierge had lit a single candle in every window of the towers and castle and throughout all of the side outbuildings.

Everything was white, except for the candles' flickering yellow flames.

In a way, the castle I had dreamed of became our home that night. Thinking about it now, I still feel the energy of that moment.

Rudi took a long, deep breath.

We looked at each other with tears in our eyes.

As we walked toward the door, our dog Juno, a brown German shorthaired pointer, came to meet us. Rudi said he had a similar type of dog when he lived in Russia. Meeting the dog in the snow made him think of his childhood.

He walked ever so silently through all of the rooms—it was a night I'll never forget.

Whenever I see his photo or hear his name, it all comes back—
the slow car ride, the unexpected surprises, the textile-covered boxes
waiting to be unpacked. The fog outside and the rare, white snow.

I was deeply sad when I heard he had died.

I was invited to attend the funeral at the Palais Garnier in
Paris. I remember that an ensemble played early music by Bach
and Tchaikovsky during the service. I remember seeing all of his
friends standing in silence along the famous staircase. I remember
the tears that fell as six male dancers carried the simple wooden
coffin away. I remember the way he could leap through the air
and make time stand still.

The Story of the Parquet

While renovating the castle in the mid 1980s, I dreamed of creating a study with a beautiful floor. I asked many people if they knew of any great parquet available. Through a referral, I heard there was something special in the north of Paris.

After a lot of difficulty with the directions, I finally found the address, which turned out to be nothing more than a garage. The seller showed me a single square piece of parquet with a geometric design. Without seeing the rest—on an impulse—I bought the entire floor.

A few weeks later, the parquet was delivered to the castle. It was much more beautiful than I could have expected. The designs used a mixture of walnut, rosewood, and maple to make intricate and unique shapes inspired by geometry, with expert precision.

We worked hard to install the floor in the study. We laid the entire parquet in place, and it was almost exactly the size that we needed, just three panels short of completely filling the room.

I have always been lucky to have skilled craftsmen in our workshop who were also knowledgeable about geometry. They made the missing three pieces. It was tremendous luck; the study I had dreamed of was a success and I thought that was the end of the story.

Some time later, our home was published in *Architectural Digest*. The article included photographs of my study. A French official saw the images and recognized the parquet. He called an attorney and they paid us a visit.

I was in total shock.

They claimed that the parquet had been stolen from a chateau in France.

I told them the story about how I found it and presented the original invoice. But they insisted the parquet had to be returned to France.

I had bought the goods legally, in good faith with the seller. These types of stories can be easily manipulated and misinterpreted, so to avoid any trouble I agreed to send it back. Arrangements were made to return the parquet to France.

During that time, the craftsmen in our workshop worked hard for many months to recreate each square. On the day that the parquet was removed from the castle, we replaced the entire floor with our version. The process of producing it was excellent technical training for our craftsmen. I consider their work to be a masterpiece.

Months and months later, I heard that the parquet had indeed been stolen from a property in France. Someone in the owner's

Axel's study with the custom-made parquet.

family was incriminated in selling the floor out of their family's castle for profit.

In the art and design business, forgeries, fakes, and stolen goods have existed throughout history. They're a problem that stretches to every corner of the art world. Selling stolen goods is a crime, and, in the end, I was grateful the truth was revealed.

Ledoux Paneling

After we moved to the castle, May and I started an annual tradition to host our company's staff in the courtyard for a pre-summer drink. The date we chose every July was the last day of work before the summer holidays. On that day in 1986, I received an offer that I couldn't refuse. A dealer from Germany called late in the day to say they had rare wooden paneling for sale near Cologne.

Because of our planned staff celebration, I hesitated, but in the end I convinced a colleague to drive with me to take a look. I told the dealer that we could come, but only very late in the evening. I think it was nearly one o'clock in the morning when I finally saw the beautifully painted paneling. I fell in love and bought it at once. It was the middle of the night by the time we got home. Although our holiday started later than planned, I was grateful for the last-minute trip.

A few weeks later, I was in London on a business trip. Whenever I had any free time, I visited the great English bookshops to consult books on architecture and design. On that trip, I found a book on Claude-Nicolas Ledoux and was astonished to see an image of the grand salon of Maison Hosten on rue Saint-Georges in Paris. In the image, I saw the exact paneling that I'd recently bought.

The photo caption said the paneling was part of the salon until about 1892 and was attributed to Jean-Siméon Rousseau de la Rottière after designs by Ledoux. The Maison Hosten had been destroyed and the original paneling was thought to be lost. What we had found was a great discovery.

I decided to have the panels gently restored and only superficially cleaned, because I loved the old patina. The work was finished just in time to exhibit at the Paris Biennale in September 1986.

When the paneling was installed at the Grand Palais, a few dealers made generous offers. But I preferred to offer the paneling to existing clients and, thankfully, I had the chance shortly thereafter. May was walking in the aisle next to our stand when she bumped into a curator from the J. Paul Getty Museum. Upon May's invitation, the curator visited our stand and admired the Ledoux paneling. The Getty acquisitions committee decided to purchase it for the museum's permanent collection.

A few years later, the Getty also acquired an early seventeenth-century Flemish display cabinet, known as a *Toonkast,* for their permanent collection. It's a fascinating piece made with walnut and oak veneered with ebony and tortoiseshell. For several years before the Getty bought it, May and I loved having the cabinet in

Doors by Claude-Nicolas Ledoux from a paneled room at the
Maison Hosten, which Axel presented at the Biennale des Antiquaires
in 1986 and sold to in the J. Paul Getty Museum.

the Vlaeykensgang. However, when we moved to the castle, for some reason I couldn't find the right place for it. The cabinet and paneling found their home at the J. Paul Getty Museum in Los Angeles.

Flemish *Toonkast*, early seventeenth century,
now in the J. Paul Getty Museum.

Jan Vlug and the Ivory Cup

For many years, I have been interested in scientific and esoteric works of art, particularly turned ivory objects. Starting in Germany in the sixteenth century and continuing elsewhere in Europe in the seventeenth and eighteenth centuries, the act of carving turned ivories was a prized form of contemporary art. Scientists, engineers, and artists made them to demonstrate their knowledge of geometry, as well as mastery of their art. Machines were invented specifically to create intricately turned models. The objects were often collected to display in cabinets of curiosities.

The act of turning ivory was a favored pastime for kings, princes, and other nobility, as well as for monks and religious figures as part of their educational studies. It was a philosophical and scientific exercise. They would meet to study the object and try to understand how it worked. They admired the techniques employed and the object's message. The slowly turned figure represented overcoming life's difficult challenges, and striving to achieve balance and harmony. Like rotating planets within the solar system, turned ivory objects were seen as cosmic symbols, which fascinated me. I saw the idea of cosmic power swirling upwards and the effort of humanity to respect the knowledge and mystery of the world.

It is often forgotten that art that we now consider old was made by artists to reflect questions about the contemporary world they lived in. I love that an element of the craftsmanship of turned ivory pieces exists in the anonymity of the maker. They are conceptual, scientific objects made by artists whose individual names were not always attached to the work. It was a shared quest of curiosity and philosophical advancement.

Throughout my life, as often as I could, I have tried to acquire antique sixteenth- or seventeenth-century turned ivory objects, because they represent the important ways that artists reflect their contemporary world. I'm firmly against the looting of ivory and the modern trade, so it's important to be sure these pieces are hundreds of years old. In historical terms, these were exotic pieces that make us look at the artists' vision and the way they gave materiality to their ideas.

My all-time favorite turned ivory object was one that I saw in the collection of our friend Jan Vlug.

Jan was a collector, tastemaker, interior decorator, and designer. He had a singular style, which earned him many interesting clients. He had great knowledge and an intuitive feeling for art. He was a big man, and what he matched in his physicality was a

Turned ivory cup,
Germany, sixteenth to seventeenth century.

larger-than-life style. He could create living spaces with antiques and old objects that were adventurous, expressive, and modern.

He liked the finer things in life—he loved the best wines and the best clothes. Whenever I saw him in London, Belgium, or around Europe he was immaculately dressed in tailored suits, colored socks, and classic tweed ties in bright colors.

He and his wife lived in a charming house accessed by a private courtyard on rue de Naples in Brussels. Their home was eclectic and full of fascinating objects—as much Asian as European—that he displayed one on top of the other. They had architectural marble floors and a marble library on the first floor where he displayed his collection. They also had a Magritte and a life-sized portrait of a white horse by Roelant Savery that I admired. He had a knack for finding old things that looked contemporary. He knew how much I admired his style and I often went to visit him for advice and inspiration.

For several days following one visit in particular, I couldn't stop thinking about a sixteenth-century piece of German turned ivory. I loved its unexpected asymmetry, craftsmanship, and technical precision. It looked like a miniature cosmos. Unable to get it out of my mind, I decided to pay Jan an unexpected visit.

After a short conversation, he asked me, "Did you come for the ivory cup?

"Yes," I said. "How did you know? Would you ever consider selling it?"

He paused.

"I know that you understand the piece," he said.

He continued to tell me that, as he got older, it became more important to him that people understood the works in the collection that he had amassed over the years.

"To you, I'll sell it," he said.

He quoted a rather significant price. Coincidentally, he had had his entire collection estimated for insurance reasons earlier that day and he offered it to me for the appraisal price.

I accepted and vowed to never sell it again.

Over the years, I've worked with clients like Yves Saint Laurent, Pierre Bergé, Lily Safra, and others on their collection of turned ivory objects and other esoteric curiosities. Clients have often admired the Vlug piece, but I've always kept it in the castle's library.

When Jan passed away, I visited his home one last time to pay respects to his family. His wife thanked me and said that I could choose any of Jan's ties that I wanted—the beautiful, English woolen ties that I had admired over the years. I couldn't decide which one I liked best, so she gave me all of them. I wear the ties in winter and think of him.

He was a contemporary man who defined good taste and found timeless style by looking at the past.

Nicolas Landau

Nicolas Landau was one of the great dealers of the twentieth century. He invented the modern version of the amateur cabinet of curiosities in the manner of European princes during the Renaissance. He was truly an original.

Landau studied law in Paris and became an antiques dealer in New York when he fled the devastation of World War II. He was a survivor.

He lived his life and built his trade in service to others, helping other families with the Jewish cause in mind. He returned to Paris where he became known as Le Prince des Antiquaires. He collected everything from scientific instruments to *vanitas*, objects of curiosity, trompe-l'oeil paintings, turned ivories, jade, silver, and other treasures. He was a tireless researcher, philosopher, writer, traveler, and intellectual.

Because of his wit, charm, wisdom, and keen eye, he was revered. All of the other dealers I knew looked up to him. His legacy has been a great inspiration in my life and collection. Together with Jan Vlug, I consider Nicolas Landau to be a mentor and master in good taste.

Regrettably, I never had the chance to meet him in person. He passed away in 1979. My friend George Van Damme introduced me to Landau's widow Madeleine. Every time I was in Paris I went to visit her at the apartment on rue du Cirque where she and Nicolas had lived together.

I'll always remember seeing the apartment for the first time. I fell in love with a collection of ancient hand sculptures that were placed on top of their piano—Roman hands, Greek hands, and even nineteenth-century hand models.

A new discovery hid within every corner of their home. They had everything—Louis XIV furniture, European seventeenth-century sculpture, *Kunstkammer* objects, archaeological artifacts, and out-of-the-ordinary *insolite* paintings. In the entrance hall, there was a stunning collection of porphyry. There was beautiful wooden paneling along the walls, and behind each panel were hidden cabinets that contained shelves lined with treasures.

When I visited Madeleine, she opened the cabinets one by one. One was full of mounted rock crystal. One was full of blue-and-white china. Another was lined with turned ivories in many different sizes. One cabinet contained only pieces of early jade. Another had ancient Egyptian stones, vessels, and vases in the type of composition that Landau was known to create. One cabinet was full of Louis XIV silver only.

Nicolas Landau in 1962.

There was simply nothing like it.

I knew that other art lovers, curators, and dealers visited Madeleine as well, seeking information and inspiration. Over time, she began to sell things to me every now and then. Each object she sold was often expensive, but the Landau eye for quality and provenance was unmatched.

Over the years, I visited her in Paris whenever my schedule permitted. Each time I arrived with flowers from the same flower shop.

One day I was running late for our appointment. I was in doubt whether to buy flowers first or go directly to the apartment and not keep her waiting. I went straight to the apartment.

She opened the door and said, "Où sont les fleurs?"[6]

I never made the same mistake again.

The last time I went to visit Madeleine she must have been in her nineties. She was as nice as ever, but something was off. It wasn't the same; she seemed tired and forgetful. She still opened the paneling and offered to sell objects, but, rather than the prices I was used to, she offered everything for very low amounts.

I couldn't believe it. I didn't want to believe it.

With those prices, the entire collection could be bought for the price of a single object in the old days. I was afraid that the next dealer to arrive might sense a bargain and take advantage of her. It became clear that she might not be able to manage the collection. The house would be empty within weeks, if not days.

---

[6] "Where are the flowers?"

Composition of a backgammon board with ivory marquetry,
Germany, seventeenth century; a terracotta hand, Italy, eighteenth century;
and a lingam stone, India, nineteenth century.

I called my friends Alexis and Nicolas Kugel, fifth-generation antiques dealers in their family's famous Galerie J. Kugel.

I explained the situation and asked for their advice. They immediately agreed to help. They enlisted a relative's assistance and, after reviewing Madeleine's condition and discussing the situation, a notary placed a block on future sales and saved the collection.

We were relieved.

After Madeleine died, I learned that she had donated the collection to the Israel Museum in Jerusalem. It was an inspiring example of purposeful philanthropy.

I was happy that the collection would be well cared for.

I think it was more than ten years later when the museum staff contacted the Kugel family and me to let us know that they didn't have the resources to house the collection as planned. It was disappointing news, but it came with a request for help.

They said that we could buy the collection from them and the proceeds would be donated back to the museum. Of course we agreed to help. We arranged to have an estimate generated for everything and completed the terms of the sale. It was a bittersweet moment. I thought about the honor and legacy of the Landau family, as well as the memory of stepping in to preserve the collection for the first time.

We decided to create an exhibition in Paris in homage to Nicolas.

Through photos and from memory, I recreated the famous Landau apartment on rue du Cirque. It was artistic, luxurious yet unpretentious, and intellectual; it exuded quality. The rooms and everything in them had a layered, musical character—it was a magical atmosphere that sang.

Axel's homage to Nicolas Landau
for an exhibition at the Galerie J. Kugel, Paris, in 2006.

We reinstalled the furniture, art, and objects to capture the original, unforgettable spirit. I wanted to recreate the feeling for visitors. The exhibition arrived to great acclaim and success.

Nicolas Landau was one of my heroes and an example of a true Renaissance man. He left a remarkable legacy of how to live with good taste. He combined his cultural wisdom with a philosophy of living life surrounded by interesting things. Even though I never met him, his legacy taught me how to look closely. He taught me how to be endlessly fascinated by the world and to share the beauty of what it contains.

Mon Dvaravati

It took me forty years to build a collection of five Mon Dvaravati sculptures. The best sculptures we have came from the collection of Dr. Jos Macken. Intuitively, I was drawn to them, even before I knew the story of their origin.

The sculptures were created by the Mon people who left India and established the Dvaravati kingdom in northern Thailand beginning in the sixth century. The Mon were followers of Theravada Buddhism and played an important role in introducing Buddhism and Buddhist art to Southeast Asia.

They lived and traveled in relative isolation; because they were perceived as a threat to the established state religion, they often were forced to flee. In their isolation, they developed a distinctive artistic style, originally influenced by art of the Indian Gupta Empire and post-Gupta styles.

The Mon Dvaravati Buddhist approach was a pure, non-dogmatic and monotheistic philosophy. It was not by killing or waging war that the Mon Dvaravati established their culture. It was through pilgrimage from their original homes in India as they traveled east in search of enlightenment that they evolved. Their journey to freedom is also symbolic; they were creating a new beginning for Buddhism in a new part of the world. It was a quest for peace, enlightenment, and friendship.

The sculptures are made in stone, the torsos draped with a tight, monastic robe. The clothing is simple and there is no jewelry. Every aspect has been considered. The smooth stone and curved contours of the genderless bodies convey harmony and proportion. With minimal material, these sculptures have a powerful presence.

Absent of decorative elements and superficial details, these sculptures, to my eye, convey something universal. They could have been Egyptian or Asian. The stone, carefully reduced to its essence, is an expression of wisdom and silent reflection. I see the appearance of a universal spirit, the mere suggestion of the human form engaged in meditation.

I was grateful to learn about the sculptures from Dr. Jos Macken—he's a significant figure in my life, like a professor who opened his classroom and shared his knowledge with me. In some ways, I consider him to be my master— a spiritual father.

Jos was a neurologist by trade and a collector at heart. He had an excellent eye. He collected abstract and impressionist paintings, Japanese screens, Chinese ceramics and jade, and Asian sculpture. He taught me to understand the differences between Chinese, Japanese, and Korean traditions through art. Jos was

One of the Mon Dvaravati sculptures,
seventh to eighth century, in the industrial space
with solid concrete columns at Kanaal.

passionate about music as well and played a Bösendorfer piano, which May and I now have in the castle.

Like many Belgians, Jos loved great wines and had a collection of the best Burgundy. But he rarely entertained at home. He accepted our invitations, but, after his wife died, he felt lonely and didn't like to receive guests. He spent his time reading. He was wise in the ways of the world and intelligent in the practice of life.

As he aged, he became fearful of the future and insecure about the expense of life and the value of his collection. I wanted to help and I promised to honor his work. I bought Jos's collection and gave it a new home at the castle. He was proud when he saw it.

He showed me the ways in which art helps us to discover the world outside of our own experiences. What I see in the sculptures now is what I felt when I saw them for the first time in Dr. Macken's home. By seeing what's absent, you feel what's present. To live with art is to give your mind space to find peace.

Jef Verheyen and Urbino

The first time I saw a Jef Verheyen painting, I was at Dr. Jos Macken's house. It was the end of the 1960s and I immediately fell in love. Jos believed in Jef's talent and was a passionate collector of his paintings, which fit very well in Jos's collection of abstract, impressionist, and Asian art.

Jef was a painter of light and color. He had a workshop in Antwerp on the Hoogstraat, which was right around the corner from the Vlaeykensgang. I often visited him there. Our friendship continued when he bought a house and moved to Provence with his wife Dani.

Jef was born in July 1932, which meant that he was younger than my parents' generation and fifteen years older than me. We had an instant connection; he became my mentor and we developed an intense friendship. In many ways, I was his pupil as much as his friend. Soon after we met, he gave me a book on proportions, which explained sacred geometry and the golden section. He gave me many books over the years, but it wasn't simply a gesture of kindness—he wanted me to study. He asked me to read the books he gave me and to write him letters about what I learned. I wrote long letters outlining my thoughts. Whenever he returned to Belgium, he came to visit and we would stay up all night drinking and talking about philosophy, art, and esoteric ideas. He was very well read and passionate about many things, including medieval art and knowledge. Jef talked a lot about the concept of the void, as derived from the Zero movement. It was an interesting combination with Jos, because Jos approached the concept through his background in Asian philosophy and art.

Jef introduced me to the Zero group and thanks to him, I became friends with Günther Uecker and his friends and contemporaries in the art world, including Heinz Mack, Otto Piene, Gotthard Graubner, Roman Opalka, as well as collectors Gerhard and Anna Lenz. His friendship opened my eyes and expanded my world. He taught me how to understand and appreciate art in new ways.

Jef was well connected in the avant-garde movements between Paris, Milan, and Düsseldorf in the 1950s and 1960s. He was a great friend of Lucio Fontana's. He wanted to introduce us, but we couldn't make it happen before Fontana died in 1969. I bought my first Fontana through Jef when I was only twenty-two years old.

I started collecting Zero art as well as Jef's work, but it was never easy. He didn't want to have a gallery and he often sold work as soon as it was made. He preferred to sell paintings directly to clients himself.

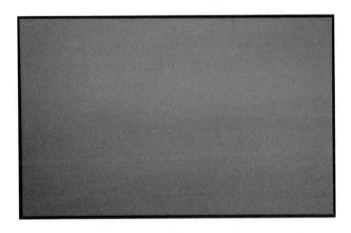

Jef Verheyen, *Urbino—L'Espace Idéal*, 1978.

In the 1970s, I organized an exhibition for him in the Vlaeykensgang and invited all of my clients and friends. All of the work was sold quickly, even before the opening.

About a year or two later, I organized a second exhibition. We hung all of the paintings and I was so honored to be able to show the absolutely beautiful work. I congratulated him and insisted that we work together on the price list.

"No, we can't," he said.

I insisted. "We must have it ready this time. I've sent out the invitations."

"We don't need it. All of these paintings are sold," he said.

He told me that he had shown the works to my clients who had bought his work in the past and these had subsequently been bought. I couldn't believe it.

"Don't worry, Axel," he said. "I'll give you a little present for your trouble."

As shocked as I was, it wasn't a problem. I worshipped our friendship. I wouldn't let anything come between that.

He was very strict with me and could be brutally honest about what he liked or didn't like about me, and I always accepted it. I saw what happened when others didn't accept his opinions. Jef was a great judo player, but often he took his judo with him off the mat. If anyone confronted him in a café and said they didn't like his art, he would grab them and throw them to the other side of the bar. Thankfully, our disagreements were only verbal and even then it was hard to win.

Once he insisted that May and I visit him in the South of France. I had so much work, but he wouldn't take no for an answer.

May and I boarded a long overnight train to Provence. We arrived early in the morning in Avignon and Jef came to the station to pick us up. I still remember the beauty of the sunrise that morning as we drove toward the house he shared with his wife Dani. It looked like one of his paintings.

He made us stop at a café where we were served the strongest coffee imaginable. When we arrived at their house, there was no one around. Jef had insisted so forcefully that we come for a visit, we assumed that they would have a big breakfast prepared to welcome us. There was nothing. May and I were dreaming about bread. I worked up the courage to ask him about breakfast.

"There's only champagne," he said.

May declined, but I accepted.

As Jef showed us to our room upstairs, we heard a loud noise as we passed the sitting room. Dani was vacuuming. She didn't say hello. We walked inside and she just looked up at us and continued vacuuming.

May and I went up to our room. We could hear Jef and Dani arguing downstairs. After the long trip and effort to get there, I felt so unwelcome. Suddenly I had a severe pain in my chest. Everything felt like it was being ripped apart. The cramps worsened until I was ready to collapse.

I asked May to call the doctor. I told her I felt like I was going to die.

Jef heard us talking and shouted from downstairs, "Come on May. Let Axel rest. He's not gonna die. Let's go out."

They left and, even though it felt impossible, I slept it off.

I knew that Dani and Jef had an intense hot-and-cold relationship and I was used to the extremes. Jef had little money when he started painting. Dani was a ceramic artist and supported them with her work.

In the beginning, they lived opposite the Rubens House in Antwerp and Dani had a shop where she sold her ceramics. When I first met her, I knew that she was a real connoisseur.

Some time thereafter, I showed her a small, twelfth-century white Sung cup that I had recently bought. I was really proud of it and thought she might like to see it, so I presented it to her after dinner one evening.

She took one look at it and crushed out her lit cigarette inside the cup.

When Jef started painting, she had stopped making pottery to ensure that he would continue. As he became more successful, the sight of pottery became unbearable to her.

Even when they lived in Provence, Jef often came to Antwerp. I think it was to escape the tension they sometimes experienced together at home.

Jef came to visit on the night that Dick was born in early June 1977. When Boris had been born a few years before, I had commissioned a painting from Jef, and I was happy that he was there for the birth of our second son.

He brought with him to the clinic a beautiful, deep purple monochrome painting as a gift. He called it *Fiori Oscuri* (Dark Flowers). The title is symbolic of many conversations we had over the years about hidden esoteric knowledge.

Axel and May's sitting room in the Vlaeykensgang, circa 1979.

I told him *Fiori Oscuri* reminded me of painting in the Renaissance and so it needed to have a Renaissance frame. We went to the Vlaeykensgang and I found a sixteenth-century wooden frame that was exactly the right size. Jef was so pleased with the coincidence. He wanted to celebrate; he wanted to buy me a drink in honor of our new son.

I accepted and, as usual, we got carried away talking all night long. It was early the next morning when I returned to the clinic to be with May. We had a private room with two beds. I took off my shoes as I entered the room so I wouldn't wake her. I climbed into bed and immediately fell asleep. May was already awake to nurse Dick. She overheard the head nurse in the hallway giving directions for the breakfast service. The head nurse told the other nurses on duty to skip our room.

"Her husband just arrived and he's sleeping now, so please don't disturb them."

May couldn't believe her ears. She had given birth the day before and was, once again, dreaming about breakfast.

On another occasion, I went to visit Jef in his studio and saw the most beautiful of his works I had ever seen. I told him how much I adored it.

"You can't have it because it's already sold," Jef said.

"It's a shame," I said, "because I love it. It reminds me a lot of Urbino."

"What did you say?"

"It makes me think about Urbino."

"Okay, that's it. You can have the painting. I'll cancel the other buyers. You deserve it."

Axel and May in front of *Urbino—L'Espace Idéal* by Jef Verheyen.

He showed me the back of the painting. He had already written *"L'espace idéal—Urbino" (Urbino—Ideal space)*. It was a remarkable, but inevitable coincidence. Jef and I had talked about Piero della Francesca over the years and the *Ideal City* of Urbino. To us, the painting represented endless light—the perfect harmony between man and the cosmos.

Urbino—L'Espace Idéal will always be my favorite Verheyen. Jef's work moves me like that of few other painters I know. Gerhard Lenz said that Jef is the Mozart of painters. He was a masterful painter of light. His canvases transform space. You don't see color in his work—you feel it with your eyes.

Jef died in 1984. Dani had been diagnosed with cancer and we were all worried about her prognosis. But then, suddenly, Jef passed away. He was practicing judo against a younger opponent and suffered a massive heart attack. He died on the mat.

On the twentieth anniversary of Jef's death in 2004, we had a retrospective exhibition of his work, and afterwards May and I hosted a feast at the castle in his honor. We invited family and friends. When it was dark, we lit a big bonfire, which burned for hours until the yellow flames disappeared in the sky.

The Princess and the Hand

One day, the Italian ambassador to Belgium called and asked if he could arrange a tour of the castle for a prominent woman visiting from Italy. On the day of her visit, I was struck by her peaceful presence, kindness, and noble manners. I wasn't surprised to learn that she was a Thai princess.

Before she left, she asked if I could visit her in Rome.

"I have a few things that I'd like to show you," she said.

She told me that her first husband was a former diplomat in Thailand, but she had remarried an Italian count and moved to Rome. She said her Italian husband couldn't bear the presence of the Asian objects in her collection.

"I've been traveling around Europe to choose the art dealer to whom I should sell my possessions," she said. "I think you might be the person."

May and I arranged the trip and arrived at the princess's home, which was a spectacular palace in the center of the old city. She showed us remarkable things, including a burned Buddha figure with a serene expression and a Sukhothai bronze hand. The long, sculpted fingers and tapering hand represented the Buddha's gesture of protection and fearlessness, but also peace and friendship. It was the most beautiful hand I've ever seen.

I knew that I would always keep it.

We agreed on the sale. When the time came to remove the hand from her home, I was unsure of how to proceed. I asked the princess if she could find a moment when she felt it was best to deliver it.

When it arrived, I was astounded.

I believe it's one of the gems of our collection.

I love the process of finding a home for things. Making clients happy, and helping to make their home the happiest place for them and their families to live, is what I love. I've learned to accept the same for myself. Sometimes the home the object seeks is my own.

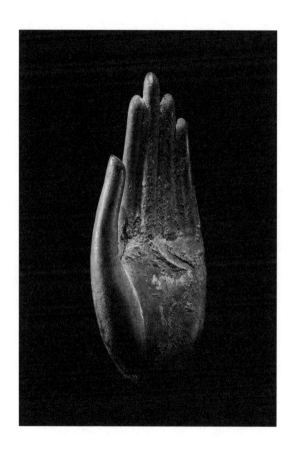

Sukhothai bronze *Hand of a Buddha*,
Thailand, fifteenth to sixteenth century.

A Dialogue with
Günther Uecker

For many years, I wanted to add an early work by Günther Uecker to our family's art collection. I've known about Uecker's history as an artist for a long time and followed his career closely. Since he began in the 1950s, Uecker has been a pioneer.

In 1958, Uecker joined Heinz Mack and Otto Piene for the first Zero exhibition entitled *The Red Picture*. It was the beginning of his collaboration with the avant-garde Zero group, and, when it ended, he built a long and prolific career.

Nails are part of his signature artistic language. Uecker hammers them onto canvases layered on wood to create sculptures and relief works. Jef Verheyen introduced me to Uecker's works and encouraged me to acquire one, but I always hesitated. I felt the nails were aggressive. Standing in front of the work, I felt something violent in the expression.

But, then my point of view changed.

As a person and a friend, I have a deep admiration and love for Günther. In his youth, Judaism and Taoist, Islamic, and Buddhist philosophies fascinated him. I suppose that's why his warmth and big smile remind me of a monk. His kindness and sensitivity are infectious and so is his optimism. I think that we share a familiarity in the sense of our approach to life—we're both inspired by Eastern philosophy—and that makes me feel close to him.

One day, while discussing his work, Günther told me that hammering nails onto the canvas is like planting trees. They rise from the canvas and transform light. It's a form of protection—protection for the environment and for the world. When he was growing up during World War II, the place where his family lived was under attack. Uecker covered the windows of the family's house with wooden planks, using nails to hammer them shut to shield his sisters and mother from the fighting outside.

As an artist, for him, the ritual of repeatedly hammering nails onto the canvas is an act of protection, healing, and purification.

This conversation changed my mind. Now, whenever I see the work, I see his process as a meditative act. The long, repetitive gesture is like a mantra performed as a personal offering of peace to the world.

In 2011, around forty years after the exhibition in the Vlaeykensgang, Boris opened a gallery in the same space where I had held the show for Jef. He chose to inaugurate the space with an exhibition of Uecker's work, as a tribute to my relationship with Jef, Günther, and the Zero artists.

I'm grateful that Günther's work is now part of our collection.

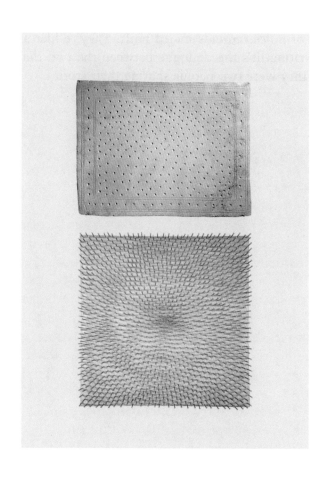

Top: Double-sided cosmogram stele,
Ecuador, Valdivia culture, second millennium BCE.
Bottom: Günther Uecker, *Struktur*, 1966.

Great art is timeless. One of Uecker's works hangs in the castle next to a four-thousand-year-old Valdivian stone tablet, in which the series of holes reminds me of nails. They're like an ancient form of writing. It's the dialogue between the two that inspires me—as if they were two people sharing their stories.

Cy Twombly
and a Change of Heart

I saw Cy Twombly's work for the first time in an exhibition at the Whitechapel Gallery in London in 1987. The comprehensive exhibition included paintings, works on paper, and sculpture. I had a strong reaction—unfortunately, it was more like repulsion.

I feel embarrassed to think about it now, but at that time I disliked everything I saw. Normally, when you don't like something, it's easier to just forget it and block it out of your mind. But, somehow, I knew I didn't have the full picture.

I couldn't fight the urge to return to the Whitechapel a short time later. I wanted to have a second look, but initially my feelings remained unchanged—I couldn't get around my negative reaction. I continued to look, and, all at once, I had a breakthrough.

I saw the work with new eyes. It was like listening to a strange language and then suddenly being able to understand. My mind changed completely and I started to love it. One work in particular gave me the key. Drawn toward the freedom of the gestures and the subtle power, I saw Twombly's work as an ancient form of writing. It was pure poetry, loaded with meaning. I've been attracted ever since.

Some months later, I saw a small "blackboard" painting in a saleroom in Antwerp. I was so enthusiastic that I bought it at auction for an amount much higher than the original estimate. I remember that it received some attention in the local press, because of the price that was paid, as well as criticism of the work itself.

Soon after, we were preparing to participate in our first art and antique fair in New York. I needed fantastic works and the Twombly was perfect. At that time, I also had a portrait of Jeanne by Modigliani. I was attracted to the idea of presenting the two paintings together, because I thought they had something in common. Each expressed a certain rawness mixed with poetic sensibility. The canvases shared a common language, one that was full of expressive storytelling. Both of the paintings were acquired quickly—the Twombly became part of a prominent English collection and the Modigliani went to Japan.

Cy was a great collector himself. I often saw him in Maastricht when he visited our stand at The European Fine Art Fair, TEFAF. Over the years, he bought archaeological artifacts from us, and he visited May and me at the castle. He walked through the castle and gardens very quietly, like he was trying to capture the energy of everything that he saw.

I remember asking him, "Cy, would you like to stay overnight?"

"It's a good idea that I stay," he answered.

Weight in the form of a sleeping duck,
Mesopotamia, late second to first millennium BCE.

We had a wonderful weekend together and the memory feels like a gift.

One of the last times I saw him was at TEFAF. He was interested in an ancient artifact, a Mesopotamian duck weight, circa 1500 BCE. Made of marble, such weights were used for measuring commodities traded in local villages.

He wanted to buy it, and I wanted to deliver it to his house in Italy personally. It was always difficult to reach him to make the travel arrangements. He rarely used the phone. His home in Gaeta was in a remote, hillside village on the coast between Rome and Naples. The best way to contact him was to call a local café, which he went to at the same time every day.

I rang him a few times, but unfortunately we were never able to fix a date in our agendas and the delivery never happened.

Some time passed.

I had heard he wasn't feeling well, as he had had cancer for several years.

In 2011, the news arrived: he had died in a hospital in Rome.

In remembrance of him, I didn't want anyone else to have the marble duck. Today, it has a special place in the library of the castle and I think of Cy whenever I see it.

Throughout my life as a dealer and collector, I have been buying art and objects constantly. I always fall in love with things; it's in my nature. Sometimes, when you're buying and selling, you have weak moments when you need money to follow your heart and support your business.

I've heard there is a French saying that describes my profession as the *métier de regret*—the profession of regret. Sometimes you miss your chance. Sometimes you make the wrong decision. Sometimes you love things, but then you have to let them go.

I don't believe it's the profession of regret.

To me, it's the profession of discovery. The thrill I have today is the same as it was when I was a teenager setting off into the world. It's the pleasure of discovery and the excitement of working with people to give things a better place. That's something I'll never change my mind about.

An Impromptu Evening
with Rostropovich

Semyon Bychkov and his wife Marielle Labèque are longtime friends of ours. Both are world-famous musicians—Semyon is a conductor and Marielle is a pianist who plays with her sister Katia. Attending their concerts and counting them as friends has been a great joy in my life.

One of Semyon's mentors and close friends was the late Mstislav Rostropovich—he was among the greatest cellists of the twentieth century. One day, after Rostropovich had recently bought a new Mercedes, he wanted to put some miles on it by taking it for a long drive from Paris. He called Semyon and asked him for advice on where to go. Semyon told him to visit the castle of 's-Gravenwezel.

"I'm sure you'll like it," Semyon said.

Rostropovich agreed.

Shortly thereafter, May and I received a phone call announcing his visit. We were told that he had come for a tour and would possibly have time to stay for lunch.

He ended up staying for two days.

He arrived about midday, and I gave him a tour of the castle, the outbuildings, and garden. May prepared lunch for all of us in our favorite spot in the garden at a table underneath an apple tree. During lunch, Rostropovich looked happy and said that he was in love with the place.

Honored by his reaction, I thought he might like to stay a bit longer. I asked if he would like to stay overnight and meet our friends. He thought it was a great idea. May and I organized a dinner that evening in his honor.

Of course, it was a challenge to invite guests with only a few hours' notice, but that was also part of the excitement. We asked several friends, including landscape architects Jacques and Peter Wirtz. I knew that Peter was a musicologist, with a particular knowledge of Shostakovich. I remember the dinner and evening included conversations about the magic of performance and the power that music has to change lives.

Over the years, May and I have received hundreds if not thousands of visitors. Some of the guests have been celebrities—famous for their business or creative talents. For our family, the castle is our home. It's the epitome of the work we do. For everyone who sees the castle, we want to give a window into our way of life. It allows us to appreciate our own experience with fresh eyes. Through the spirit of sharing, it remains a humbling experience to think that, by inviting guests into our private world, we can offer inspiration to others.

Stones and Silence

I keep twelve small stones next to the castle's swimming pool. I collected them on various trips or received them as gifts from friends. They are stones that I find beautiful or interesting. Each stone has a distinctive story and meaning.

For example, one stone represents wisdom, another represents proportion, and another one is a symbol of intuition. A triangle-shaped stone represents spiritual life. I collected one stone on a mountainside in Japan and, when I look at it, I see a symbol of Eastern philosophy.

I collected other stones on the beach in Greece and in the mountains of Switzerland. I've taken one from the coast of Palm Beach—one side of the stone represents intelligence and the other side represents roots. One stone came from Bhutan and represents happiness.

Each time that I swim, I use the stones to count the number of laps and I arrange the stones in a new composition. At the end, I concentrate on what I see. Based on the arrangement of the stones and their meaning, each composition delivers a new message. It helps me know what will be important for the day. It's a simple routine that provides the ability to seek inspiration from nature. It offers awareness.

I believe stones are created by time and carry the power of the earth. Stones are like silent, slow-living animals—they have a spirit that resonates for thousands and even millions of years.

I believe there is a distinctive spirit in different types of stones—my practice is a reminder of that. It's a way of giving nobility to an earthly object that looks humble, but actually has weight and meaning.

In our workshop, I have designed floating stone tables using black Belgian slate. The creative process includes simply running my hand over the stone, not to give it the shape that I want, but to respect the shape the stone has already—like its hidden soul—and to use this as a guide in the design. Creating a patina by rubbing our hands over stone objects can be a healing process.

One of my favorite gardens is the stone garden at Ryōan-ji, the Zen temple in Kyoto. Completed in 1450, it's a masterpiece of doing a lot with very little. The dry landscape is arranged in a rectangle, bordered at the far end by an earthen clay wall. The colors of the wall are made by time, faded to a rusty orange and dusty brown.

Stones with a message arranged along the edge of the castle's pool.

Large rock formations appear to be swimming in a sea of perfectly combed small pebbles. There is a trace of moss surrounding the stones. But there's no water—instead, there is an endless void defined by its absence.

Rather than trying to explain what cannot be explained, I think less of the garden's meaning and more about the meditation it inspires. The garden teaches respect and restraint and shows us purity and simplicity. It's a place of silence and peace.

A Branch in a Vase

Some of the most inspiring trips in my life have been to Japan. I love the Japanese spirit, which is expressed in gardens and art. Even when I'm extremely busy, I make time to cut a branch or arrange flowers in a vase. It's relaxing and inspiring, like a meditation practice.

Over the years, what I've learned to do with one branch is to create a sense of unity and calmness. The ideal process is to know your purpose. You should know the vase you intend to use and then go for a walk in nature.

Try to find a branch that, once it has been cut, will improve the plant or tree. Perhaps it makes room for other branches or gives more space for the plant to grow and thrive. By trimming a tree or a plant, you can make the whole system lighter. I'm attracted to branches that have had to work hard to grow. I have a tendency not to choose a branch that grows straight and high above all the rest. I like a branch that's heavy and appears as though it has been struggling.

Sometimes, I have to look for a long time before I find the perfect branch, but the search is rewarding. A kneeling or bowing branch is nature's design—a symbol of time passing, a symbol of humility that adds harmony to the environments of life.

A single branch placed in dialogue with
a Shiro Tsujimura ceramic work.

Drawing from Observation

In the 2000s, May and I became members of The Prince's Drawing School. It was founded by HRH The Prince of Wales and later became The Royal Drawing School. The school helps students of any age learn the art of drawing and hopes to restore the language of drawing as a fundamental creative practice.

May and I had accepted an invitation to Windsor Castle to attend what became an unforgettable evening. As the date approached, I was surprised to receive a phone call to ask what I would like to see when visiting the castle. The Royal Collection at Windsor is one of the best art collections in the world—it's vast and full of masterpieces.

What would I like to see? That was a big question. I wasn't sure if I should even dare to ask, but I said I would love to see some

Renaissance drawings, by artists like da Vinci and Raphael, and perhaps even a few Holbein portraits.

The organizer responded, "Okay, I've made a note of it. I'm not sure if it's possible, but we'll try to arrange it."

When we arrived for dinner, we were ushered into a series of small, intimate libraries. Each library had a central table that was surrounded by shelves on all sides. The first table I saw was covered with drawings by da Vinci. I was awestruck by the technical genius. In the drawings of the human body, he was a master at conveying scientific knowledge with subtle gestures that contained so much power and skill. Another library was full of drawings by Raphael—one masterpiece after the next. There were several tables covered with treasures from the collection—each library was as fascinating as what came before.

In addition to Prince Charles's vision of drawing as a classical art that needs to be preserved, I admire him for many reasons, including his charity work, environmental initiatives, and supportive vision for culture, urban planning, and architecture. In our private meetings, he is personable and down-to-earth, with a charming personality and warm sense of humor.

May remembers sitting next to him during a dinner at Buckingham Palace when he showed her his rough hands from working outside. They talked about their mutual passion for gardening and growing vegetables.

One of the most beautiful parties we have ever attended was a sponsored charity event at Buckingham Palace. Because of the grandeur and size of the palace's rooms, I thought the feeling inside would be cool, if not a little bit cold. It was exactly the opposite.

The atmosphere was warm and inviting. As we exited the car and walked up the stairs through the entrance, we passed a grand red hall with two lit fireplaces.

We were escorted inside the State Rooms, and passed glasses filled to the brim with champagne. Next, we entered the long, majestic Picture Gallery where the guests were gathering for dinner. A live orchestra played the music of Purcell. We walked around the room, surrounded by masterpieces I had only seen in textbooks and catalogues. Works by Titian and Vermeer hung alongside paintings by Rubens and Van Dyck.

We were guided through other State Rooms and salons, before entering the Music Room. Dinner was served at a series of round tables, and each table had a silver-gilt centerpiece, ornate china, and intricate flower arrangements. We listened to the Orchestra of the Age of Enlightenment accompanied by singers performing Handel's "Hallelujah" chorus. It was one of those evenings in which art, music, and beauty have the power to take your breath away.

Discovering Gutai

For more than twenty years, May and I hosted visitors over two weekends in the spring and fall; this became a tradition among antiques dealers in Antwerp, in order to share their newest discoveries. Often, on very busy days, we would receive thousands of visitors to the castle.

In the spring of 2005, I was standing at the entrance when a man that I didn't know approached me. He said that his name was Tijs Visser and he was the curator for the Museum Kunstpalast in Düsseldorf.

Mattijs "Tijs" Visser had come to the castle that day for an appointment with our team to discuss an exhibition he was organizing. He asked me if he could borrow some of the artworks from our collection for his exhibition on Zero and Gutai. I didn't know what he meant by Gutai. I invited him to sit with me on a small wooden bench inside the castle's entrance gate to explain. There he began to tell me, for the first time, about the Gutai Art Association. This conversation expanded my views on art and changed my life.

Hundreds of visitors streamed past us as he told me the story of Gutai. I should have been greeting the arriving guests, but I was transfixed by the conversation.

He explained that the word Gutai means "concrete" or "concreteness" and that the Gutai Art Association was Japan's most influential avant-garde art group, comprising artists who worked from the late 1950s to the early 1970s, and whose driving manifesto was originality. Gutai's founder, Jiro Yoshihara, urged the group to "do what no one has done before!" Gutai is about freedom: freedom to speak, freedom to act, freedom to create. I was fascinated by every detail.

"If you're excited about Gutai," he said, "then perhaps you'd like to join me on a trip to meet some Gutai artists?"

Tijs was planning to travel to Japan in August. His schedule was packed with meetings with Gutai artists or their surviving family members. His goal was to arrange installations and live performances, and to borrow works for the exhibition in Düsseldorf.

I agreed immediately. He made me promise on one condition.

"That you'll join me at Koya-san," he said.

Koya is a mountain range near Osaka, and the headquarters of a Japanese Buddhist sect founded by a monk named Kukai in the ninth century.

I was ready to make my plans. There was only one scheduling problem. Tijs booked his trip the same week as the due date for the birth of our first grandchild. I knew that I couldn't go; I wanted to be home when the baby was born.

Kazuo Shiraga, *Suiju*, 1985.

Thankfully, Tijs agreed to postpone the trip from the end of August until the beginning of September. We proceeded with the travel arrangements. I was thrilled at the chance to learn as much as I could about Gutai.

On the day of our departure, the baby still hadn't been born. I called Dick to check on his wife's status. Marleen was feeling well and they didn't expect the birth to happen soon. They would keep me posted.

We departed for Japan. Our schedule was full of appointments.

We met Shozo Shimamoto, Sadamasa Motonaga, and Kazuo and Fujiko Shiraga. We planned to meet Atsuko Tanaka, but unfortunately she was not well and was unable to receive our visit. (Sadly, she passed away the following year.)

Every second of every day, I fell deeper in love with Gutai. Seeing the artwork was a revelation. After each meeting with an artist or their family, I couldn't believe that Gutai artists were little-known outside of Japan. I vowed to do everything that I could to raise their profile and increase awareness about the artists and their revolutionary work.

One of the enduring memories from that trip was the chance to meet Kazuo Shiraga. Seeing his work for the first time was a total shock. I was overcome by its power and beauty and felt it deep in my chest.

I knew a bit about his life story. I had heard that he spent some years living in a Buddhist monastery, which had a big influence on his work. I thought, therefore, that we would have to visit him in a humble village in a remote mountain location. On the day of our appointment, I was surprised when our car approached a wealthy suburban neighborhood near Osaka that was full of big houses. I thought it was a mistake.

As we walked toward one of the biggest houses, I said to Tijs that he could ring the doorbell, but I was sure that it wasn't the right house. We were surprised when a staff member opened the door and invited us inside.

There was a small Zen garden surrounding the house. We were led towards an entrance salon and asked to remove our shoes. I looked around the room and saw a collection of decorative treasures—lacquer boxes and gold screens. It was not at all the idea I had had of what the Shiraga's home would look like.

After a few minutes, we were led into an adjacent space. In the center of the room, two chairs were placed facing two others. Tijs and I sat down. Kazuo Shiraga entered the room and sat directly across from Tijs. His wife Fujiko took the chair opposite mine. Atsuo Yamamoto—scholar, curator, and longtime supporter of Gutai—knelt beside the Shiragas to translate.

Looking at Kazuo was like gazing at a mountain—strong and silent. I watched Fujiko's noble gestures and refined manners. The pair had a powerful presence.

Both were artists and often worked together.

Kazuo meditated on the empty canvas, until, at once, his body seemed to explode with a burst of energy. To execute his paintings, he suspended himself from the ceiling with a rope, using his feet to spread paint across the canvas.

Fujiko applied the paint. Together they decided when a work was complete. These powerful gestures on the canvas are like traces of cosmic energy.

During the conversation, we discovered that Kazuo was a member of the Japanese Zero group, which was founded in 1952 or 1953. Tijs wanted to know what the group's name meant and if it was different from the European group.

Tijs explained that, in German, the word for "zero" means "the beginning."

Kazuo said that zero was the point where you come back and start again.

Later, Fujiko showed us her works on paper, which she had made by pressing her hands and feet on wet paper until the paper became damaged and wrinkled. She showed us one of the last works she had available, which was made at the end of the 1950s. From then, she had stopped producing independently to support Kazuo in his work.

I was interested in one of her historical works. It consisted of a single 32-ft. (10-m) wooden plank that she had cut down the middle. The original piece had disappeared. We asked if it would be possible to recreate this work for the exhibition. Because of her age, she was no longer able to saw the wood herself.

There was a brief silence while she considered the question.

I felt it was the right time to tell her how interesting I found her work. I said that her work related to the process of uncovering the path ahead. She used the fullness of her material to carve out an empty space, a void that creates a new world. When I finished speaking, I wasn't sure how she would respond. The room remained quiet.

Our conversation moved toward other questions Tijs had for the Düsseldorf exhibition. At the end of our visit, Fujiko went to her workshop and got her handsaw—the exact one she had used to saw the original plank.

Fujiko Shiraga, *Shiroi Ita* (White Board), 1955.

With Atsuo's help, she asked if I would cut the plank for her. I was so moved by the experience, I couldn't hold back my tears. When I looked at Tijs, I saw tears in his eyes. Fujiko was crying, too. With great honor, I accepted.

I took the saw home to Belgium and, during a period of two weeks, I sawed a wooden plank in half to create the exhibition copy, which was later destroyed.

I was honored to pay tribute to her work.

Throughout the trip, every appointment gave us an enlightening new experience. We visited Saburo Murakami's widow. I bought an iconic work from 1957 entitled *Peeling Picture*, which symbolized a concept that would later develop into the *Artempo* exhibition.

We visited Sadamasa Motonaga, who lived in a colorful contemporary house. Motonaga's work with water, stones, candles, smoke, and air maintained the playful, humorous, and original tone that founder Yoshihara encouraged in the Gutai group.

We visited Tsuruko Yamazaki's home on the seventeenth floor of a residential building and I bought early work from her. I was in awe of her style—she was almost eighty, and her nails and eyelashes were painted a bright shade of turquoise. Simple and elegant, she served us three small pieces of orange on a small, round plate.

We visited Shozo Shimamoto. He showed us many great works of art, including a work that he had made in the early 1950s using layers of newspaper piled on top of each other. He threw objects through this new type of canvas, creating holes that revealed the emptiness behind the work. His first work was made by accident, but founder Jiro Yoshihara loved it.

Saburo Murakami, *Peeling Picture*, 1957.

During our first visit I was able to buy a hole picture from 1954, as well as other historical works, directly from Shimamoto.

At around the same time, in Europe, Lucio Fontana was causing a revelation in the art world by making slashes in the canvas to reveal the third dimension—the empty space behind the canvas. It deepened my belief in the originality of the Japanese Gutai artists' work. Gutai needed to be an important part of the universal conversation about the postwar, avant-garde art movement.

This trip put me on a path of discovery.

I wanted to meet as many Gutai artists as I could. It was my goal to create an exhibition and make a book on Gutai art.

Before long, I returned to Japan to meet Yuko Nasaka, Tsuyoshi Maekawa, Norio Imai, and others. Over time, I continued to develop relationships with other artists and their families, like Masatoshi Masanobu, Ryuji Tanaka, and of course Sadaharu Horio and Kazuo Shiraga.

On the first trip and those that followed, I started acquiring every historical piece that I could buy. It was the best thing I ever could have done, but I didn't realize it at that time. I didn't know that the members of Gutai and their revolutionary art would become well known so quickly.

Within ten years, the museum exhibitions *Destroy the Picture: Painting the Void, 1949–1962* curated by Paul Schimmel at the Museums of Contemporary Art in Chicago and Los Angeles, and *Gutai: Splendid Playground* curated by Alexandra Munroe and Ming Tiampo at the Guggenheim in New York dramatically raised the international profile of Gutai. These were in addition to the exhibition Tijs curated with Jean-Hubert Martin at the Museum

Axel in the castle library in front
of *Concetto Spaziale* by Lucio Fontana, 1959.

Kunstpalast in 2006 for the show *Zero: International Avant-Garde Artists in the '50s and '60s.* It was a groundbreaking show.

In the meantime, during my first Gutai trip, I phoned home every day to check on the news of the birth of our first grandchild. Each day passed with no news.

One day, Tijs finally took me to see Mount Koya.

We hiked until we reached a small, humble hut.

As the monks believe that their founder Kukai is not dead, but still alive and meditating for hundreds of years awaiting the arrival of the future Buddha, we watched as candles were lit and food was offered at the door. As we stood in front, I wasn't prepared for how moved I would be. It was a spiritual experience for me—much stronger than I ever thought it would be. I felt Kukai's presence.

Tijs and I walked down the hill in silence. We arrived at the little village to have dinner in a local restaurant. I had the feeling that I should try to call home once again. I wanted to share the news about visiting Mount Koya.

May answered my call.

"Our granddaughter is born," she said. "Her name is Kay."

I was overjoyed.

In that moment, I promised myself that I would return to Japan with my granddaughter Kay to see Mount Koya. In 2017—together with her parents, her sister Yasmine, her brother John, and my wife May—that's exactly what we did.

Mount Koya in Japan.

My Way of Wabi

Jef Verheyen and Dr. Jos Macken taught me to be focused and intense. They taught me to be strong and seek connections to nature.

Nature is our greatest master. They said that I must find a reason for everything that I do and seek to express that reason. They told me never to be decorative—to avoid it at all costs. To be decorative is to do things just to please others, to create beauty for the sake of beauty.

With their influence, in my twenties I began to study Chinese Taoism, Japanese Zen Buddhism, and Korean philosophy. It led me to seek connections between Eastern and Western philosophy. Through the simplicity of Zen's spiritual insights, I discovered the concept of *wabi-sabi*, the Japanese aesthetic in which beauty is found in things that are humble and imperfect.

I met Leonard Koren and read his book *Wabi-Sabi for Artists, Designers, Poets, and Philosophers*. I read Junichiro Tanizaki's *In Praise of Shadows*. The elusive concepts of *wabi-sabi* started to become clearer.

Everything came into a sharper focus when I met the architect Tatsuro Miki (known to his friends as Taro). I knew Taro's father, Ryoichi Kinoshita, through Dominique Stroobant, who is a mutual friend. Ryoichi is a prominent architect in Japan and an expert in traditional wooden structures.

Their family's famous expertise with traditional Japanese architecture was invaluable when I started to work on a project near Bruges for a close friend. In the course of the project, we had the idea to build a *minka* on the property—a humble house that was traditionally the home of merchants, artisans, and farmers. We wanted to draw connections between the similarities of traditional Flemish architecture and traditional Japanese architecture. We wanted to create a style where East meets West—a geographic and architectural dialogue that would create a new language.

We asked Taro for help—he has lived and worked in Brussels for more than twenty years. He suggested that we travel to Japan together to search for the perfect *minka*.

It was the beginning of a long collaboration and the start of many trips that we would take together over the years. He has taught me a lot about Japan and taken me to places I had never been before, while introducing me to artists and artisans—which are one and the same in Japan.

We quickly realized that the two of us shared many of the same philosophies. In our work, we have both been searching for the

Japanese *minka* brought to Flanders.

universal link between East and West. Seeing Europe and Asia through each other's eyes has broadened our perspectives.

We searched for a word that could outline our approach—the term *Wabi* was adopted almost by chance. The spirit of Wabi—adopted from the ancient Japanese aesthetic *wabi-sabi*—embraces the spirit of thinking globally and acting locally. It's about embracing the essence of materials and valuing everyday human interaction.

Once we found a name, we wanted to define and document the qualities we felt were the most Wabi—simplicity, humility, purity, nobility without sophistication, and the beauty of imperfection and incompleteness.

We decided to create the book *Wabi Inspirations* to help share this idea with a wider audience. We added photographer Laziz Hamani and writer Michael Paul to the team. The book's success was surprising. It taught me that Wabi speaks to people of many socioeconomic backgrounds because it allows them to find an expression in their daily lives, no matter how or where they live.

My way of Wabi is a return to the lessons I learned earlier in my life, which took me decades to express. Wabi is accepting that time is both an observer and creator. Wabi is a return to nature.

The castle's Wabi room.

Sunbi Spirit

While working on the book *Wabi Inspirations*, Taro and I were searching for connections between East and West. We wanted to build bridges between different geographies and discover links between the past, present, and future. We studied historical architecture in Korea and Japan. We quickly realized that traditional Korean architecture was also close to what we felt was the Wabi spirit. The rough, natural look of Korean houses contrasted with the refined details of traditional Japanese houses.

Looking at design and architecture wasn't enough. We wanted to see the places where the traditional Korean spirit lives and breathes in today's world. We wanted to look outside of museums. To do so, we needed a local guide.

I spoke with Bien-U Bae—a photographer, scholar, artist, and friend. I was certain that he would have a good suggestion. I was surprised when he said that he wanted to guide us himself. In 2010, together with his daughter Youngji, the four of us planned a ten-day trip.

We visited Gyeongju, a coastal city and former capital of Silla, one of the world's longest-serving dynasties. We visited royal tombs and hiked in the neighboring pine tree forest, which Bae had photographed.

We visited Yangdong, a folk village full of traditional houses where we met the descendants of aristocratic families who still lived there. We went to Jeju Island to visit ancient homes and see local villages. We explored Jeju Stone Park and studied the history of stone culture.

One of the most inspiring moments of the trip was in Haeinsa, a Buddhist temple located deep in the Gaya mountains, built in the year 802. We slept overnight in the temple residence, which reminded me of a cloister. I remember the night was short and cold. The morning was full of magic.

We woke up at 4 a.m. for the day's first chanting and prayer service. We walked in silence to and from the service, while heavy snow fell around us.

I learned that Haeinsa is the home of the *Tripitaka Koreana*—the entirety of Buddhist scriptures carved onto 81,350 wooden printing blocks in the thirteenth century.

A part of world heritage, the canon includes some of humanity's greatest knowledge. It is stored in a series of library buildings constructed from the most basic materials: stone, wood, and earth. I was touched to see the simplicity of these spaces and learn about the wisdom they contain.

Axel at Haeinsa temple in Korea, in front of the library buildings
that house the *Tripitaka Koreana* sacred Buddhist texts.

Our quest to see the traditional spirit of the country led us to discover nature through its rivers, mountains, islands, and forests. We observed life in the monasteries, villages, and big cities. A major impact on my personal work and philosophy was my learning about the Sunbi people and the Sunbi spirit.

Sunbi means a "man of virtue." It's the name for Korean aristocrats who embodied Confucian ideals. The Sunbi pursued a noble existence by means of public service, social justice, and the continuous pursuit of knowledge through study. Their goal was not to gain skills or to achieve success, but to change communities by promoting peace. They lived a discreet life full of respect for others and in harmony with nature. Although the Sunbi were part of a noble class, they lived modestly, with sophistication and refinement.

Sunbi is a spirit and a state of mind. This idea deepened my understanding and appreciation for Korean artists in the Dansaekhwa movement—such as Chang-Sup Chung, Seobo Park, and Hyong-Keun Yun. Sunbi is a way of finding beauty in bare simplicity. It's about living life free from artificiality. It's about seeking nobility through the purity of scholarship; by surrounding yourself with objects that are minimal and restrained, with an inherent respect for nature. It's a truth that I want to bring to my own life.

Moon Jar by Dae-Sup Kwon.

Tariki Hongan

Ichi-go, ichi-e is a Japanese expression that means "Each moment is unique." I first learned about the concept from Taro and from my three Japanese artist friends—Sadaharu Horio, Raku Kichizaemon XV, and Shiro Tsujimura—who helped to deepen my understanding.

The literal translation of the phrase is "One time, one meeting." It's a reminder of the ephemeral nature of everything around us. Every meeting and every creation presents an infinite number of possibilities. You can take the same trip or get together with the same people, but it will be different every time. It's similar to the idea that you can never step in the same river twice, because the water is always changing.

Taro taught me that, in the sixteenth century, Sen Rikyu, Japan's famous tea master, emphasized the meaning of *ichi-go, ichi-e* in his work. He had an eye for beauty and simplicity and was responsible for furthering the concept of the wabi tea ceremony. He reduced the size of the tearoom to the most essential space. He eliminated material things. Through the rituals of the tea ceremony, he affirmed the idea of a spiritual interaction between people. He valued the type of beauty found in imperfect and irregular objects, often in their most natural state. He focused on austerity, selflessness, and finding peace through simplicity.

In 2007, we visited a gallery in Osaka and saw an exhibition of work by Sadaharu Horio. I wasn't surprised to learn that Horio was a member of Gutai; he had joined in 1966. His work has the same creative, free spirit. His work, as his life, is performance. He transforms things we see in daily life—scraps of metal, wood, used paper, junk—into spontaneous art to show us that every *thing* is unique.

I liked everything in the exhibition. I asked the gallery owner how many works were available. She said that Horio had recently moved from a bigger house into a smaller one—as he now had less storage space, there were many works available.

She showed me images of everything and I made an impulsive decision. I wanted to buy the complete collection. The gallery owner was hesitant.

I explained my belief in the work, which was growing every second. Luckily, one of Horio's friends, Mr. Shimizu, was there to call Horio and invited him to join us. He told Horio that I was an art lover, dealer, Gutai collector, and new fan of his work. He encouraged him to trust me.

From left to right: Tatsuro (Taro) Miki, Axel, Akiko and Sadaharu Horio
in the Horios' home in Kobe, Japan.

"Your work will be in good hands with Axel-san," he said.

"Okay," Horio said, "let's do it."

Horio calls the process of everything that he makes *atari-mae-no-koto*, which means "a matter of course." Every work is what it is. It's less about the final product and more about the creative process and the original, spontaneous, and playful act of creation. For Horio, artworks aren't created to communicate an idea or position about the world or the artist. To live in the moment is to experience the world around you. To create something is to honor the truth of that experience.

One night, Taro and I were having dinner in Osaka with Horio, Gutai scholar Koichi Kawasaki, and a group of close friends. During the evening, Horio said that as he gets older, he has even more ideas for his work. There are many new things he wants to make, more things that he wants to do. But he recognizes that, at his age, he can't do anything alone. It's only through the help of his team and his friends that he can realize his ideas. His dreams are possible because we believe in him.

"Axel, you are *tariki hongan* to me," Horio said.

Taro explained that *tariki hongan* is a Japanese expression that comes from Zen Buddhism. Its original use was related to strength and enlightenment through prayer and meditation. But its meaning has changed over time.

The way *tariki hongan* is popularly used in Japan today—and what Horio was trying to express—means "putting oneself in the hands of others" and "relying on the power of others to realize your dreams."

Sadaharu Horio's live performance *Atarimae-no-koto*
at the Axel Vervoordt Gallery in Antwerp, 2011.

Horio said that I represent *tariki hongan*, because I believe in his work. He thanked me for the encouragement, which gives him the creative energy he needs in his later years.

"Alone I am nothing," he said.

I have the same feeling. I need my family, friends, and colleagues to help me realize my dreams.

A few years ago, Horio made a performance for the *In-finitum* exhibition at Palazzo Fortuny using ordinary paper that we had found in Venice.

The works were stunning and original. One of our colleagues recommended that we try to find the best materials possible for Horio to use in his work, rather than making do with what was available. We wanted Horio to make things that could last for an eternity.

Taro, with the help of a friend, Mr. Shimizu, and an artist, Shimakawa, discovered a source of the finest paper available. They found it in Fukui, where paper is produced with a special herb using a method that was developed over a thousand years. Picasso bought the same paper for his work. Shimakawa said the paper was sacred and divine. Unlike other papers, which are made with wood pulp and become sour or disappear from exposure to light, this paper lasts hundreds, if not thousands of years.

We presented the paper to Horio. Through live performance, he transferred his energy onto the paper and permanently captured a moment in time. He has taught me that singularity exists in every second.

On another trip to Japan, I met Raku Kichizaemon XV, the patriarch and current head of the Raku family. His wife, Mrs. Fujiko Raku, is a friend of Taro's mother, and she arranged for us to meet.

The Raku name follows an uninterrupted line of fifteen successive generations of ceramicists—dating back more than four hundred and fifty years. They make the traditional type of pottery used in the tea ceremony. It began with a commission from Sen Rikyu in the late sixteenth century, for a black tea bowl made by Chōjirō, the first Raku in this family's long line of potters.

Over the years, the techniques and secrets have been passed down from father to son. Once the son is ready to accept the work, he inherits the Raku title and keeps the family's tradition alive. Each generation is a gateway to the next.

I admire the way the family inherits the burden of tradition, particularly Raku XV, and accepts this duty with a sense of freedom. They rely on the strength of others that came before them. Each Raku lived, learned, worked, shared their secrets, and built a bridge from the past to the present. In a way, they've made a single work created over time.

After this first meeting, we quickly became friends. The Raku family has visited us in Venice and Belgium, and May and I have visited them many times in Japan. We've met Raku and Fujiko's two sons—Masaomi, the youngest, is a sculptor, and the eldest, Atsundo, has accepted his destiny to become Raku XVI, the next generation.

Raku XV designed a contemporary tea pavilion that is part of the Sagawa Art Museum in Moriyama, Japan, one of my favorite museums in the world. Water surrounds the outside of the museum.

To reach the tea pavilion, you have to walk down a flight of stairs. You can see the water through a glass roof, and it gives you the feeling of being submerged in another world.

If you look at the first black Raku bowl ever made, it's simple and unsophisticated. Some would even say it looks too humble, even meagre. That's exactly what I love. It has the Wabi ideals of transient imperfection. Raku pottery is connected to nature. It's a link to the past. Sometimes Raku pottery looks like a living creature—prehistoric, otherworldly, even cosmic. A work by Raku shows us that we all have the ability to see the universe in a flower, a stone, a piece of wood, or a simple bowl of tea.

Shiro Tsujimura is another Japanese potter who reminds me that every moment is unique. I was aware of his work, but I never had the chance to meet him. Hiroko Horiuchi, a great family friend, suggested that I arrange to visit Tsujimura's home in the mountains outside of Nara the next time I was in Japan. She said that I would love it, and, of course, she was right.

I'd seen his work in exhibitions, as well as museum collections, so I was surprised when I walked toward the house and saw pottery buried in the grass all around the dirt path. Everywhere I looked on the property, there were ceramics partly buried in the dirt or resting on top of the ground.

I quickly learned that it was part of Tsujimura's process. He puts his pottery outside in the sun, wind, and rain. The works age with nature and through exposure to the changing seasons.

Inside the house, we were invited to join Tsujimura to sit on the burnt-black wooden planks on the floor in the living room.

Raku Kichizaemon XV, *Yakinuki tea bowl*, April 2016.

He cooked fresh vegetables and meat over hot coals on an exposed grill in the center of the room.

His wife Mieko prepared soup and other dishes in the kitchen next door. Everything was served on dishes made by Shiro. He poured a great red Burgundy from a curved spout in a deep bowl he'd made.

I was in awe of Mieko's gentle smile and noble gestures. Over the years of our friendship and during the many times I have visited them, I always have the best dinner with them. There is a simple, elegant hospitality that is impossible to recreate.

Tsujimura is a free spirit and his practice is self taught. I feel connected to him for many reasons, not the least of which is that we were born in the same year. He started to create pottery around the same age as I was when I bought the Vlaeykensgang. He developed his own traditions. When he was young, he built the house and studio himself. There were gaps in the walls, and some of the rooms had no heat. As he became more successful, he and his wife have upgraded their surroundings, but they've always lived in the same house.

On one of my trips to their home, I fell in love with one of the kiln misfires. Tsujimura had pulled the pottery out of the kiln after it cooled, and several pieces were collapsed and stuck together. The clay had expanded like permanent glue, and the individual pieces became one mangled and magnificent piece—the art of an accident.

As an artist, he accepts his place as the in-between person. He creates with earth. The fire transforms it. He has the choice to throw it away or accept it. He was surprised when I told him that I loved it.

"It is what it is," he said.

Ichi-go, ichi-e.

Shiro Tsujimura's works at his studio
and home near Nara, Japan.

Celebrating Life

Giving a big party is a chance to celebrate life. In a way, it's like buying a painting. But one that you never sell and that no one can ever steal. No one can ever take the memory of a great party away from you.

Looking back, after forty years, I realize that every ten years there has been a reason to celebrate life.

1977: Renaissance Party at the Vlaeykensgang

During one of my buying trips to England in the 1970s, I was sitting in a car and I asked the driver to go slowly as we passed a small shop. I saw a bright gold cupboard in the window. The style of the cupboard was baroque and nineteenth-century, but in the center I noticed a much older detail, a part with rock crystal and precious stones.

I quickly asked the driver to pull over.

I ran inside the shop. I needed to see the cupboard up close.

Looking at the middle of the cupboard, I could see details that were characteristic of a typical Renaissance cabinet. I saw rock crystal, semi-precious stones, and a variety of marble and *pietra dura* inlaid into ebony. Everything I saw was of such exceptional quality that I bought the cabinet at once.

When the cabinet arrived at our workshop in Antwerp, we dismantled it. The nineteenth-century gold cupboard was built like a frame around another cabinet that was much older. We removed the frame and saw that the interior cabinet was indeed made in the seventeenth century. Looking at the gold cabinet was like looking at the cover of a book and opening it to find a completely different story inside.

On the doors of the seventeenth-century cabinet, there were royal portraits painted on stone (see page 105). There was an engraving of a coat of arms with a crown and the initial E.

Through research, we learned that the ebony cabinet was made for the marriage of Princess Eleonora Gonzaga of Mantua to Holy Roman Emperor Ferdinand II of Austria. The cabinet was probably made in Mantua for the occasion.

What I had initially loved for its quality and aesthetics became even more appealing. It was a reminder of how our stories are sometimes wrapped up in objects, wrapped inside stories that exist within other stories.

The cabinet is a bridge through time. I was fascinated by Mantua and this period in history for many reasons.

Feast of Light celebration at the castle of 's-Gravenwezel in June 1988.

In 1608, Peter Paul Rubens returned to Antwerp after spending eight years in Italy. His Italian years began in Venice and, after he studied there, he eventually settled in Mantua at the court of Duke Vincenzo I Gonzaga.

Claudio Monteverdi was also employed at the court in Mantua during the same time as Rubens, and composed his two most famous operas, *L'Orfeo* and *L'Arianna*, which premiered in 1607 and 1608, respectively. The first was an entirely new dramatic form of music and the second is one of the most famous examples of early baroque opera, which is still one of my favorite types of music.

One of the houses I bought and renovated in the Vlaeykensgang was built in 1608. This particular building, which currently houses the Sir Anthony Van Dijck restaurant, was formerly one of the homes that was used by the Rockox family, an important family in Antwerp.

May and I met at a party at another Rockox house in the city center. Because I feel connected to the history of the Vlaeykensgang as well as my hometown, these stories have played an important role in my life.

The city of Antwerp was planning huge festivities to celebrate the four-hundred-year anniversary of Rubens's birth on June 29, 1977. It just so happened that my thirtieth birthday was also on June 29, 1977, and so when friends suggested that we throw a party to celebrate both occasions it seemed like a perfect idea.

Jef Verheyen was enthusiastic, and his ideas were a big influence when we started planning.

A boat ride at dawn on the moat after the Feast of Light.

We decided to host the party in the Vlaeykensgang and chose the theme of the Renaissance in honor of the style of that period. The Renaissance was a cultural bridge between the Middle Ages and modern life—it was a new beginning, a rebirth.

Dick was born at the beginning of June 1977 and so we decided to plan the party for the end of the year. Jef originally wanted to throw the party in June anyway and to put a four-poster bed in the center of the space for May and our newborn. He said it would be just like paintings from the old days, with a beautiful woman propped up on fluffy pillows and nursing her baby while being surrounded by friends and family having a lot of fun.

Luckily, May didn't think the idea was as appealing as Jef made it sound, so we set a date in December.

We needed many months to plan and organize. We wanted to create a setting that perfectly matched the grandeur of sixteenth- and seventeenth-century paintings. We studied what people had eaten and drunk during that period. Chef Roger Souvereyns created a menu of twenty-seven dishes inspired by the seventeenth century. I invited friends over on Sundays for Renaissance dance lessons. I had silver plates and glasses made for the occasion. I also wanted to bring back together all of the important silver pieces that I had acquired and placed in collections years before. There was amazing royal silver from the English court, like fantastic ewers, which were made by Jenkins for the coronation of Charles II. There were seventeenth-century silver wine coolers and a gilt-silver *tazza*, made in 1545 in Antwerp, which had become part of the Antwerp silver museum. We made 16 ½-ft. (5-m) buffets piled high with silver.

Axel gives a toast at the Victorian Opera Ball
at the Reform Club in London in January 1997.

Throughout the Vlaeykensgang, we paid homage to vegetables and created huge garlands and table settings that looked like still-life paintings. In one room, we hung one hundred and forty Caucasian carpets on the ceiling and old tapestries on the walls. There was a *Kunstkammer* piled high with paintings.

It was also the period at the end of the 1970s when Yves Saint Laurent was inspired by the Renaissance, so many of the women had incredible dresses—even couture YSL creations—especially made for the party.

An orchestra played early Renaissance dance music. There was not a single electric light burning in the Vlaeykensgang. Every room in the entire party was lit by candlelight. The atmosphere was pure magic.

1988: Feast of Light, Castle of 's-Gravenwezel

In the beginning of 1988, I was walking over the bridge at the castle when I felt a shock of light. It was like a flash of lightning, but the sky was clear. It was the end of something and the beginning of something new. From that moment on, my attitude toward the castle changed completely. After years of renovation and countless hours of work, I felt one with the castle. This feeling wasn't there in the beginning, but this shock of light changed everything.

That moment inspired the idea to host another big party—a feast in gratitude for the light. *Hommage en lumière.* We chose St. John's Day, the midsummer date in June, which is the longest day of the year, the day with the most light. It is six months before Christmas, which, in the Christian tradition, is celebrated as the birth of light.

From left to right: Boris, May, Axel, and Dick
at the Victorian Opera Ball.

On the west side of the park, we installed a giant U-shaped tent, 180 ft. long and 180 ft. deep (55 x 55 m). The setting and decorations were entirely white—inside and outside the tent, and even in the castle. In the library, all of the objects were wrapped in white paper. Musicians and singers performed classical music and opera throughout the night.

Katia and Marielle Labèque played a concerto by Mozart. Ballet dancers performed to Falla's *Ritual Fire Dance*. Groups of singers sang throughout the evening until sunrise.

In conjunction with the party for adults, I organized a party for children as well. Dick's guitar teacher entertained as a clown. To introduce the dessert, which was carried on an engraved throne platform, all of the children danced in a cortege to the music of *Carmen*. The dessert was a miniature castle made in white sugar, served together with many types of white sweets.

We had laser lights projected from the castle through the park to the end of the forest that were synchronized with Schubert's *String Quintet in C Major*. The party lasted until sunrise the next morning, when a group of singers performed a beautiful ode to the moon from *Rusalka*. In the morning, we boarded a boat on the moat and sailed into the new day.

1997: Victorian Opera Ball, London

Becoming a member of the Reform Club in London was a way for me to show a lifelong love for England. The club was founded in 1836. The atmosphere is unique in the world—its architectural beauty, paintings, books, and furniture are unparalleled. I wanted to share this passion with others and decided to host a Victorian

Table settings in the courtyard of the Palazzo Ducale
(Doge's Palace) in Venice in 2007.

Opera Ball in the entire club. The date selected was our twenty-fourth wedding anniversary in tribute to May, the love we share, and her role in the life of our family.

My friend Koen Kessels, who is now Music Director of the Royal Ballet at Covent Garden, selected excellent singers from the English National Opera who mixed with the guests throughout the night. Performances were held throughout the club. Friends offered Victorian silver, candelabras, and centerpieces to use for the setting and May did all of the flower decorations, which were works of art. We wanted to revive the emotional joy of opera and nineteenth-century glamour. As usual, the night was too short.

2007: Doge's Palace, Venice

In 2007, *Artempo* opened in Venice. To celebrate the exhibition and my sixtieth birthday, we invited friends for a three-day weekend. The entire experience was unforgettable. The highlight was a dinner for 488 guests at the Doge's Palace. The dinner was a charitable event designed to fund the restoration of the Palazzo Fortuny. Koen Kessels chose the music and Robert Carsen directed the party, creating the mise-en-scène and orchestrating the entire rhythm of the evening. For 488 guests seated at one long table, Robert wanted to have 244 servers, so everyone could be served at the same time.

Dries Van Noten created the look of the evening and designed the musicians' and servers' attire. Musicians played music by Monteverdi on brass instruments in the Gothic palace's grand courtyard. The spectacle was sensational and timeless, like Venice always is.

Kanaal—home of the Axel Vervoordt Company, gallery, exhibition spaces,
permanent installations for the Axel & May Vervoordt Foundation,
and private residences—was also the setting for the Arts Feast in 2017.

2017: Arts Feast, Kanaal

Every celebration has marked a next step in my life. In 2017, there were three milestones in my life. I concluded the series of exhibitions I helped curate over a period of ten years at Palazzo Fortuny. I turned seventy. And the construction at Kanaal was complete—the spaces dedicated to our company, gallery, exhibition spaces, and permanent installations for our family art foundation. It's the collaborative result of May, Dick, and Boris and me working together with our company's team to help us realize our dream to share our vision on art and architecture. We decided to organize a three-day opening to celebrate the achievement.

Like the Vlaeykensgang and castle, it's a place that represents our way of seeing the world. The Arts Feast continued the spirit of decades of celebrations to commemorate and share a joy of life with others.

Anish Kapoor:
Giving Body to the Void

In 2015, May and I took our granddaughter Kay to Lyon, France, to see an exhibition of works by Anish Kapoor in the neighboring Dominican convent of Sainte-Marie de La Tourette designed by Le Corbusier. Brother Marc Chauveau warmly received us, and when I thanked him for the tour of the exhibition, he said:

"It's not an exhibition. The works live here."

I love this expression and think of it often.

To live with art is to allow art to live with you.

At the end of the 1990s, Boris and Dick helped discover and purchase the Kanaal—a group of industrial buildings and grain silos along the banks of Belgium's Albert Canal. It took us nearly a decade to acquire the entire site.

Over the years since, Kanaal has become the home for our company's showrooms, workshop, studios, and gallery, as well as exhibition spaces and permanent installations for our family foundation.

In the physical center of the original property is a large, round building that was used as a storage space for grains that arrived by boat. It was always my intention to commission a major living artist—such as James Turrell, Anish Kapoor, or Richard Serra—to create an installation for the space. I was inspired by John and Dominique de Menil's vision to create the Rothko Chapel in Houston. I wanted to transform the industrial site into a more spiritual place—a center for contemplation and a symbol of peace.

In 1992, following a recommendation from his aunt Lia, Boris went to *Documenta IX* in Kassel, Germany. There, he saw a work entitled *Descent into Limbo* which was a hole in the ground installed in a dark room. He said that, at first, the hole looked like a flat surface on top of the ground, but, after a closer look, he saw that it was indeed a hole—a seemingly bottomless cavity that deepened beneath the floor. It was lined with a dark pigment so that the space appeared to reach an unfathomable depth. It was created by Anish Kapoor. Boris said it was the most fascinating work of art he had ever seen.

I wanted to know more about Kapoor and his work. Over the years that followed, he was an artist who was high on our radar. In the late 1990s, Boris gave me a book on Kapoor that was published on the occasion of a retrospective exhibition. On the cover

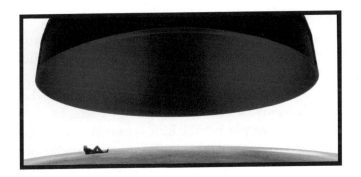

Anish Kapoor, *At the Edge of the World,* at Kanaal.

of the book was a work entitled *At the Edge of the World*. When the time came for an installation at Kanaal, I thought *At the Edge of the World* was the work we needed.

Anish is an artist who has the ability to give body to the void—to use material to show us what immateriality is. He's a sculptor of space that gives the chance to contemplate infinity by showing us a vision of full emptiness.

At the Edge of the World is an enormous dome that measures 16 ½ ft. high by 26 ft. wide (5 x 8 m). The inside of the dome is lined with an intense, deep red pigment. Standing underneath the dome and looking at the red pigment overhead, you have the sensation that you cannot see the beginning or the end of the space. It feels limitless—like a glimpse of infinity.

Anish says of the piece: "The idea is to make an object which is not an object, to make a hole in the space, to make something which does not actually exist. Even more, the extraordinary appearance, loved and feared, of a piece of void, at once finite and infinite, reactivates the symbolic contact between inside and outside, earth and heaven, male and female, active and passive, conceptual and physical, thus renewing the process of knowing."

May and I tried to see *At the Edge of the World* exhibited for the first time in 1998 in Spain at the Centro Galego de Arte Contemporánea in Santiago de Compostela. But by the time we could make it there, it was gone.

Inauguration celebration in the Escher building at Kanaal
for the installation of Kapoor's work in June 2000.

I wanted to track it down. I was convinced this work should have a home at Kanaal.

We made arrangements for Anish to visit the site and we started discussions with him and his gallery to arrange for the installation.

Anish proposed to make a different project for the space.

I didn't give up. I was convinced that this was the work we needed for Kanaal. I promised that the installation would be permanent and available for visitors.

At the end of 1999, the discussions were successful and the acquisition became a reality. *At the Edge of the World* would come to Kanaal.

The work was installed in 2000. Shortly afterward, we had a party to inaugurate the space. We invited a few hundred guests for dinner in the concrete loft inside the Escher building at Kanaal.

May placed thousands of candles throughout the empty three-story building. The guests sat at two long wooden tables. We served a buffet dinner with white and black bowls filled with pasta. Musicians hid percussion instruments in different corners of the room. Our friend Mireille Capelle performed improvisational singing inspired by the sounds of the guests in the room. The drums and her simple sounds were like an echo of the life that filled the space.

It was a moving tribute to Kapoor's work next door.

Years later, Anish returned to Kanaal. He said that we were brave to acquire one of his first, expensive monumental works. He stood underneath his sculpture with tears in his eyes. He said that he considers *At the Edge of the World* to be one of his masterpieces.

I agree.

The duality between the physicality of the work on the outside and the infinity conveyed by the inside is profoundly moving.

It's like an engine, filling the entire Kanaal site with its creative spirit. *At the Edge of the World* is its beating heart.

The work lives here.

Artempo

All of my life I've been interested in old things. I'm attracted to objects with patina. I'm drawn toward wood with scratches and marks from years of use. I love old tables and peeling paint. I love oxidized copper. I love the aged spirit of natural materials.

The twenty-first century must be a century of recuperation.

As we become more conscious of the natural resources we use in our daily lives, we must find creative ways to reuse what has been discarded. Ever since I started searching for antiques in my youth, I began to understand that to live with antiques is not to return to another period in history. I see antiques as something very modern, with a history that tells us as much about the present and the future as it does the past.

I want to accept things as they are because I understand that time changes things. The patina that objects have is a result of the passage of time, the elements of air and nature, as well as the energy from the people who used them. That's why I prefer soft restoration rather than total renovation. You can never bring something back to the way it was. Time adds a new dimension. To accept the roughness and beauty of patina is to understand that time is the ultimate artist.

This was the idea that gave birth to the exhibition *Artempo: Where Time Becomes Art,* held at Palazzo Fortuny in Venice in 2007. It was the first exhibition I participated in as a curator, and, in many ways, it was a natural evolution in my work.

The seed was first planted during the Gutai trip to Japan. It grew out of a small moment that became something much bigger. We were walking in Osaka. In the midst of a crowded city, we saw two modern office buildings rising up into the sky. In between, there was a narrow alley that led to a small, old temple. The contrast was so fascinating—the connections between public life and private spirituality, between interior and exterior, between old and new.

Through the ugliness of modernity, we saw something we appreciated in a different way. I had always been looking to find the presence of harmony, strength, silence, and spirituality in things. We talked about the impermanence of life and the beauty of imperfection—the idea of accepting simplicity and humility, and respecting the role of nature.

We became interested in the juxtaposition of these ideas—old and new and the way that time transforms and sculpts matter. Over the days and months ahead, the dialogue grew into a search for objects that looked flawed, but were full of beauty. It was an

Installation view of piano nobile during the *Artempo*
exhibition at Palazzo Fortuny, Venice, 2007.

idea that I had pursued in the past when placing an oxidation painting by Andy Warhol from my collection next to an oxidized panel that could be found on the street. I put a rough, natural stone next to a Lucio Fontana sculpture. I wanted to look at art like a child who knows nothing about art but only feels its power. I wanted to be surprised by the connections.

The idea of time and contrasts was encouraging, and Tijs Visser suggested that we combine works from my private collection and ask artists to make contributions. Tijs and I conceived the concept for the exhibition and asked Jean-Hubert Martin to collaborate. We named it *Artempo*.

The next step was to find a home for the exhibition. We wanted to stage the exhibition alongside a contemporary art fair. Once the idea of Venice was floated around to coincide with the Biennale, I went to the city to look for potential locations.

I saw many places that I loved, including old buildings near the Arsenale shipyard, but none of them had the grandeur of a Venetian palazzo.

Through connections I met Daniela Ferretti, Director of the Palazzo Fortuny museum in Venice. The palazzo was the former home of Mariano Fortuny. I loved Mariano Fortuny's life story. He did everything—painting, photography, textiles, lighting, stage design, fashion design, interior decoration, writing, illustration, and costume design. Inside the palazzo, I loved the unrestored walls and unique character that filled every floor. Fortuny's spirit felt alive.

With approval from the city of Venice, our request to host the exhibition at Palazzo Fortuny was accepted. We found the perfect

Installation view of the second floor of *Artempo*.

home to present *Artempo*—a place where art, beauty, and time intertwine.

The exhibition was an enormous critical success. We had over fifty thousand visitors and sold over ten thousand catalogues. As a first-time curator, *Artempo* changed my life. It was the start of a ten-year relationship with Palazzo Fortuny and Daniela.

During those years, six more exhibitions followed, and each lasted for more than six months. The experience led to the creation of the Axel & May Vervoordt Foundation, which helped to support the exhibitions.

Shortly after *Artempo* opened, I went to Japan with Taro and a close friend to find traditional *minka* houses for our project near Bruges. During the trip, Taro proposed to show us the former workshop of Isamu Noguchi in the village of Mure on the island of Shikoku.

We agreed, but it wasn't an easy destination. We traveled by car, trains, and boat to get there. When we finally reached the village, I saw an industrial site full of smoking chimneys. It made me depressed. Thankfully, my perception quickly changed.

Once we arrived at Noguchi's workshop, a totally new world opened. I walked in and saw thirty or forty unfinished stone sculptures. Per his request, when Noguchi died, everything was left untouched. It was a tranquil place, frozen in time. Walking through his workshop, I felt the power of each stone. I thought the unfinished ones were the most beautiful Noguchi sculptures I'd ever seen.

At that moment I wanted to do a second exhibition to explore the infinity in the unfinished. I called Daniela to explain. She immediately agreed and wanted to participate. It became *In-finitum*.

El Anatsui's work *Fresh and Fading Memories*, 2007,
installed on the façade of Palazzo Fortuny for *Artempo*.

As the plans moved forward, we realized that we needed more time to go deep into the theme. *In-finitum* required philosophical investigation. We needed an intense period of study.

This pursuit led us to another idea for an exhibition, *Academia*, which was a tribute to academic studies and the transmission of that knowledge into the creation of art.

Logically, we knew that *Academia* should come first.

I invited an intimate group of about eight people with backgrounds in science, art, philosophy, and music for a series of salons, think-tank sessions, and philosophical discussions organized around the theme. We wanted to bring knowledge and clarity to our ideas. We wanted to share our questions and expertise with one another.

It was a process that we started in preparation for *Artempo* and continued for each exhibition over the ten years that followed.

In 2008, *Academia: Qui es-tu?* debuted at the Chapelle de l'École des Beaux-Arts in Paris. Dominique Paiini from Paris, who had helped introduce me to Daniela and the Palazzo Fortuny, suggested that we place a metal grid in front of the large plaster casts in the Chapelle—which functioned as study models—and use the grid to install work by contemporary artists.

It was a dialogue between study and creation, which revealed the heart of the theme. An academy is a place of knowledge, a place of transmission, and a source of questions and answers—the identity of the intellectual combined with the soul of the artist.

A year later, in 2009, *In-finitum* followed at the Palazzo Fortuny.

The first three exhibitions—*Artempo, Academia, In-finitum*—formed a philosophical trilogy, a series bound by the art of time, in the pursuit of knowledge, and the quest for infinity.

Anish Kapoor, *White Dark VIII*, 2000, installed
in Palazzo Fortuny for the *Intuition* exhibition, 2017.

In each exhibition, we've included many works from our private collection as well as the work of the Gutai artists. It was a commitment, not only to my passion for their work, but also to my vow to bring their work to international audiences.

The next two exhibitions, *TRA: Edge of Becoming* in 2011 and *Tàpies: The Eye of the Artist* in 2013, continued the natural progression of establishing a theme and trying to understand the knowledge related to it.

TRA explored the idea of the threshold and the empty space in between two objects, which is full of an invisible energy. An important prefix and suffix in words that range from "transformation" to "mantra," *TRA* symbolized a doorway, a passage, and a journey toward initiation and purification.

Working with hundreds of artists and thousands of works of art in the first six years of the Fortuny relationship, we, the curatorial team, were able to sharpen our focus for *Tàpies: The Eye of the Artist*. This exhibition allowed us to see the world through the eyes of the prolific Catalan artist, Antoni Tàpies, through his work and personal collection that crossed boundaries, genres, and geographies. Seeing his eye as a collector gave me a newfound appreciation for his work, which I'd always loved and collected myself.

In many ways, the exhibition that followed in 2015—*Proportio*— was one that I had been working on for decades.

Early in our friendship, Jef Verheyen gave me my first book on sacred geometry. Ever since I bought the castle in 1984, I continued studying proportions and the golden section with the help of

Tori, a traditional Japanese temple gate from Shirahige Shrine, Japan;
a symbol for the *TRA* exhibition, Palazzo Fortuny, 2011.

Professor Bernard Lietaer. It became a lifelong passion of mine. The study of proportion can be approached through almost every discipline—music, science, art, architecture, philosophy, design, medicine, and nature.

I had the unforgettable opportunity to experience the timeless wisdom of proportions in the early 1990s when I took our family to Egypt.

We visited Cairo during a period of great unrest in the city. We were guests of the Belgian ambassador, and he arranged for us to visit the Pyramid of Cheops after closing time. The site was completely empty except for our guide, Boris, Dick, and me. It was absolutely magical. When we arrived inside the pharaoh's burial chamber, the proportions captivated me and we decided to measure the dimensions of the double cube space.

Proportio allowed me to share this pursuit of knowledge and passion with visitors through twentieth-century masterpieces, old master paintings, archaeological artifacts, and architectural models and books.

On the ground floor of Fortuny, Taro and I designed and built a series of pavilions with sacred proportions using hemp. We originally intended to put art inside, but, in the end, we decided proportion should be the only element present. Each of the five pavilions was built using dimensions found in sacred geometry. We wanted visitors to experience proportion physically and spiritually.

In 2017, we staged the final exhibition in the series at Palazzo Fortuny entitled *Intuition*. Through ancient artifacts and contemporary art that spanned thousands of years, we explored the mysterious

Axel and May's Venetian apartment.
On the wall, an *Artempo* circle by Axel
and a sculpture by Dominique Stroobant and Jef Verheyen.

definition of intuition—the ability to acquire knowledge without proof or evidence.

Throughout my life, I've relied on my intuition to make important decisions. I wasn't always able to explain why I made one decision instead of another. The curators and I wanted to understand the feeling that guides a person to act in a certain way without fully understanding why. Intuition connects human thought and behavior to the energy of the cosmos. In a way, this is how art is made. Every great discovery emerges out of intuition.

Each exhibition was a next step in my life. To realize the exhibitions, the curatorial and think-tank team found a concept by following our intuition. Our conversations started with a question or an idea, and often this led us toward deeper and more searching questions. Each theme provided a new source of knowledge. Becoming a curator was a way to share this knowledge with others.

Working at the Palazzo Fortuny added a profound new dimension to my work. May and I created an apartment in Venice that became a home. Daniela became like a sister to me. Curating and organizing *Artempo*, *Academia*, *In-finitum*, *TRA*, *Tàpies*, *Proportio*, and *Intuition* gave me a broader view of the world.

Intuition was both an end and a new beginning.

In 2017, construction for Kanaal was completed. The spaces dedicated to our company, art gallery, Inspiratum, and exhibition spaces and permanent installations for our family's foundation were finished. It will be the future home for more exhibitions and

A round library in the concrete silos at Kanaal.

projects. It's a way to share our vision on looking at and living with art. It was a dream that was years in the making.

Looking back, I see connections with the early days in the Vlaeykensgang and the castle—building a bridge from history to the future. Kanaal is writing its own story. It's a center for art with a life that's evolving.

I'm looking forward to what's next.

From left to right: son-in-law Michael, Dick, May, Axel, Boris, and daughter-in-law Marleen at Kanaal.

Axel Vervoordt: A Chronology

1947
Born in Wilrijk, Belgium, on June 29 to Elsa (known as Mani)
and Jos Vervoordt.

1966
Graduates from St. Xaverius College, a Jesuit secondary school.

1969
Purchases a private street with sixteenth-century houses known
as the Vlaeykensgang in the center of Antwerp next to the Cathedral
of Our Lady. Renovates the site over eighteen years and settles there
as an art and antiques dealer, selling pieces to museums and attracting
a new generation of clients.

1972
Marries May Schelkens, with whom he further develops his art and
antiques trade. Together they develop and promote a new way of living
with art. The couple has two sons—Boris in 1974 and Dick in 1977.

1982
Participates for the first time in the Biennale des Antiquaires in Paris,
where he meets prominent clients and friends and earns international
exposure. Conceived as a loft, his debut stand features an important
collection of art, objects, and furniture presented casually.

1984
- Purchases the castle of 's-Gravenwezel, which was first mentioned in historical documents in 1108. After a thorough two-year restoration of the main building, side buildings, and park grounds, the Vervoordt family moves into the castle in 1986.
- Participates for the second time in the Biennale des Antiquaires, where he surprises audiences with a theatrical stand featuring a large selection of Ming porcelain recently purchased from the Hatcher cargo collection. Continues working with prominent museum acquisitions committees, and sells Ledoux paneling to the J. Paul Getty Museum.

1998
Purchases Kanaal—a nineteenth-century industrial complex alongside the Albert Canal in Wijnegem, Belgium, near Antwerp, where he set-up up the company headquarters.

1999
The site includes offices, workshops, and showrooms where rare furniture, archaeaological artifacts, and contemporary art mingle with unique creations.

2000
Kanaal is expanded. Axel acquires and installs on-site *At the Edge of the World*, a monumental work by Anish Kapoor.

2002
- Creates Inspiratum—a music foundation that sponsors young musicians and organizes concerts with world-class musicians in intimate, historical spaces to promote music appreciation. Conductor Koen Kessels is appointed as the first artistic director and, along with Giulio D'Alessio, is responsible for the annual program.
- During the Biennale des Antiquaires, the "Kanaal à Paris" barge is installed on the Seine with an eclectic selection of furniture, antiquities, and old master and contemporary art, including installations by Anish Kapoor and Willem de Kooning. The exhibition amazes the Parisian public and marks Axel's debut with a new generation of admirers.

2004
- Holds a retrospective exhibition of Jef Verheyen's works at Kanaal entitled *Lux est Lex*; the exhibition commemorates the twentieth anniversary of the artist's death.
- Auctions off part of his collection at a Christie's house sale held at the castle of 's-Gravenwezel. The successful sale reaches a wide international audience of art and design lovers. The sale of approximately 1,000 of the nearly 16,000 pieces in the collection frees up storage space for expansion.

2005
Travels on a discovery trip to Japan to meet living Gutai Art Association members and their families. Begins collecting, promoting, and selling their work internationally. Combined with inspiration from Zero group, the trip plants the seed for the founding of the Axel Vervoordt Gallery.

2007
Surprises the art world by organizing the seminal exhibition *Artempo: Where Time Becomes Art*, held at the Palazzo Fortuny to coincide with the Venice Biennale. The exhibition debuts to critical success and marks the start of a ten-year partnership with Palazzo Fortuny, Daniela Ferretti, and Fondazione Musei Civici di Venezia.

2008
- *Artempo* is followed by a second exhibition, *Academia. Qui es-tu?*, held in the Chapelle de l'École des Beaux-Arts in Paris. The exhibition is a tribute to academic studies and the transmission of knowledge into the creation of art. *Academia* forms the second part of a continuing trilogy of exhibitions.
- Establishes the Axel & May Vervoordt Foundation, to manage the family's art collection, which ranges from antiquities to contemporary artw. It also engages in curatorial, sponsorship, and educational activities.

2009

- Focuses more time on creative pursuits: architectural works, curation international exhibitions, and travel to meet artists and collectors. Transitions leadership responsibilities within the company to his sons.
- Boris oversees the company's main activities related to art and antiques, the home collection, and interior design, promoting the business's core values—quality, durability, and harmony—and steers the company through a new phase of expansion.
- Dick oversees real estate activities and is instrumental in the creation and revitalization of the Kanaal project, bringing together private and public spaces in a shared community. With his wife Marleen, Dick develops real estate projects, including new developments and the restoration and repurposing of historic buildings, for the family business.
- Axel curates *In-finitum* at Palazzo Fortuny with Daniela Ferretti. The last in the trilogy of exhibitions that included *Artempo* and *Academia*, it explores the theme of the "infinity of the un-finished." It continues the tradition—referred to internally as *tariki hongan*— that began with the earlier exhibitions to establish a think-tank team that meets for philosophical and research discussions to provide a framework of knowledge for the exhibition.

2010

Curates, together with the Zero Foundation, the exhibition *Jef Verheyen: Le peintre flamand* at the Langen Foundation in Neuss, Germany.

2011

- Boris opens the Axel Vervoordt Gallery—a contemporary art gallery in the Vlaeykensgang, the site of his father's personal and professional beginnings. Gutai and Zero artists are part of the gallery activities, in addition to modern and contemporary artists such as Dansaekhwa and others whose spirit converges with the gallery's commitment to the concept of the void, the physical act of creation, and the experience of space and time. The gallery's work allows Axel to deepen the relationships developed with artists over the years.

- Axel curates the exhibition *TRA: Edge of Becoming* at Palazzo Fortuny with co-curator Daniela Ferretti. *TRA* explores the idea of the threshold, transformation, and the empty space in between two things, which embodies unseen energy.
- Work begins at Kanaal to transform the site, with one hundred residential units and thirty commercial spaces and offices. The architecture team includes Stéphane Beel, Coussée & Goris, Bogdan & Van Broeck, and Michel Desvigne for landscape work.

2013
Curates the exhibition *Tàpies: The Eye of the Artist* at Palazzo Fortuny with Daniela Ferretti in close collaboration with the Tàpies family. The exhibition is based on the work of Antoni Tàpies along with his personal art collection, presenting Tàpies's unique way of seeing the world through art.

2014
The Axel Vervoordt Gallery opens in Hong Kong, the gallery's second location, and continues expansion in Asia. The gallery programs five exhibitions per year and participates in art fairs in the United States and Europe.

2015
Curates the exhibition *Proportio* with Daniela Ferretti at Palazzo Fortuny, which examines the role that proportion plays in our lives through multifold representations found in art, nature, physics, economics, history, science, music, medicine, and many other disciplines. The study of proportion uncovers the natural patterns used to create everything in the material world. Attended by more than 70,000 visitors.

2017
- The Axel Vervoordt Gallery in Antwerp relocates to a new space at Kanaal, opening with a retrospective exhibition of paintings by Kazuo Shiraga, an artist whose work the gallery is instrumental in bringing to global prominence in the art world.

- Curates *Intuition* with Daniela Ferretti, the sixth and final exhibition at Palazzo Fortuny, and the seventh overall in the series. *Intuition* explores the ability to acquire knowledge without proof, evidence, or conscious reasoning—the feeling that guides a person to act in a certain way without fully understanding why.
- Opens new spaces for the Axel Vervoordt Gallery, Axel & May Vervoordt Foundation, and Inspiratum at the newly completed Kanaal, with rooms designed by Axel with Tatsuro Miki to house forthcoming exhibitions and special projects, including musical events and think-tank salons.

Awards

- Association of the Belgian Warrant Holders for the Belgian Royal Court (since November 2001)
- Knight of the Order of Arts and Letters of France (since September 2002)
- *Architectural Digest (AD100)*: International directory of 100 interior designers and architects (2004, 2007, 2008, 2012, 2015, 2016, 2017). Selected for the 2017 "*AD* Hall of Fame" honor, which highlights the world's "10 Best Interior Designers"
- Officier in de Kroonorde (since December 2008)
- *Tàpies: The Eye of the Artist* voted best exhibition by the Associació Catalana de Crítics d'Art (ACCA) in 2014
- *Proportio* at Palazzo Fortuny voted best exhibition of the year in 2015 by Leading Culture Destinations

Affiliations

- C.B.E.O.A. (*Chambre Belge des Experts en Œuvres d'Art*)
- C.I.N.O.A. (*Confédération Internationale des Négociants en Œuvres d'Art*)
- C.R.A.B. (*Chambre Royale des Antiquaires de Belgique)*
- S.N.A. (*Syndicat National des Antiquaires Négociants en Objets d'Art, Tableaux anciens et modernes de France*)
- Patron of The Royal Drawing School
- Reform Club, London
- President of Inspiratum
- Chairman of the Saint Paul's Music Chapel Patronage Committee, Antwerp

For a full list of fair participations, exhibitions, events, and publications by the Axel Vervoordt Company, Axel Vervoordt Gallery, Axel & May Vervoordt Foundation, and other information, please visit:
www.axel-vervoordt.com

Exhibition Catalogues

Artempo: Where Time Becomes Art
June–November 2007
Palazzo Fortuny, Venice
MER. Paper Kunsthalle
Published in English and Italian.

Academia, Qui es-tu?
September–November 2008
Chapelle de l'École Nationale
Supérieure des Beaux-Arts, Paris
MER. Paper Kunsthalle
Published in English and French.

In-finitum
June–November 2009
Palazzo Fortuny, Venice
MER. Paper Kunsthalle
Published in English and Italian.

TRA: Edge of Becoming
June–November 2011
Palazzo Fortuny, Venice
MER. Paper Kunsthalle
Published in English and Italian.

Antoni Tàpies:
The Eye of the Artist
June–November 2013
Palazzo Fortuny, Venice
MER. Paper Kunsthalle
Published in English and Italian.

Proportio
May–November 2015
Palazzo Fortuny, Venice
MER. Paper Kunsthalle
Published in English and Italian.

Intuition
May–November 2017
Palazzo Fortuny, Venice
MER. Paper Kunsthalle
Published in English and Italian.

Published Works by Axel Vervoordt

Axel Vervoordt: The Story of a Style
Photographs by Laziz Hamani
Assouline, 2001, for the English
and French editions.

*At Home with May
and Axel Vervoordt*
Text by Arend Jan van der Horst
Photographs by Cees Roelofs
Lanoo, 2001, for the Dutch edition.

Axel Vervoordt: Timeless Interiors
Text by Armelle Baron
Photographs by Christian Sarramon
Flammarion, 2007, for the English
and French editions.
Also published in Dutch and German.

Axel Vervoordt: Wabi Inspirations
Axel Vervoordt in collaboration
with Tatsuro Miki and Michael Paul
Photographs by Laziz Hamani
Flammarion, 2010, for the English
and French editions.
Also published in Dutch, Italian,
and German.

*At Home with May and Axel
Vervoordt: Recipes for Every Season*
Text by Michael James Gardner
Photographs by Jean-Pierre Gabriel
Flammarion, 2012, for the English
and French editions.
Also published in Dutch, German,
and Russian.

Axel Vervoordt: Living with Light
Text by Michael James Gardner
Photographs by Laziz Hamani
Flammarion, 2013, for the English
and French editions.
Also published in Dutch, German,
and Italian.

Index

Page numbers in **bold** *refer to images.*

Acknowledgments

To make this book, we began with a list that Axel made
that included one hundred moments from his fascinating
life. During a period of time that lasted many weeks,
we met as often as we could. Axel started to tell me his
stories and I learned many things that I never knew.
In the months that followed, as I listened to the recordings
of the time we spent together, it became clear that many
of the one hundred moments were connected. One thing
leads to another. One story contains many. In the end,
we agreed upon the stories that we have shared with you
in this book. It could've easily been much longer. Whether
the stories are public or private, the most important trait
that each story possesses is its personal quality. Each story
is like a door that Axel opened, allowing us to see a new
room and inviting us inside.

There were many people involved in the creation of this
book. I would like to thank the following people for their
contributions:
Kautar Abidine, Bien-U Bae, Youngji Bae, Tom Bovyn,
Semyon Bychkov, Annelies Castelein, Luc Derycke,
Martine Dornier, Anne-Sophie Dusselier (and family),
Jean-Pierre Gabriel, Becky Gardner, Chris Gardner,
Betty Gertz, J. Paul Getty Museum, Laziz Hamani,
Chioly Kasugai, Alexis and Nicolas Kugel, Katia and
Marielle Labèque, Evelyn Lauer, Robert Lauwers, Anna Lenz,
Jan Liégeois, Metropolitan Museum of Art in New York,
Tatsuro Miki, Royal Museums of Fine Arts of Belgium,

William Nedved, Michael Paul, Veerle Pauwels,
Hedwige Speelmans, Günther and Jacob Uecker,
Sir Anthony Van Dijck restaurant, François Van Schevensteen,
Frederik Vercruysse, Patrick Vermeulen, Mattijs Visser,
Jeroen Wille, and Lieven Winkels.

I would like to especially thank Boris Vervoordt,
Dick Vervoordt, and Natascha Van Deun. You were there
every step of the way and generously offered your time
and expert reader advice. You steered this project with your
heart and your incredible help. I'll always be in your debt.

I would like to offer my utmost respect to Kate Mascaro
and Ghislaine Bavoillot and the entire team at Flammarion.
I'm humbled by the opportunity to work together.
Your expert guidance, enthusiasm, perfectly timed feedback,
as well as your experience and professionalism taught me
a great deal. I'm forever grateful.

My love and thanks to Marleen De Wolf and to May
Vervoordt—who is like a family historian. Thank you for
opening the fascinating photo archives and offering your
precious time whenever I asked for help.

And to Axel, you have my deepest gratitude and appreciation.
The time we spent together talking, laughing, and telling
stories has been one of the great privileges of my life.

—**Michael James Gardner**

The editors Ghislaine Bavoillot and Kate Mascaro express their deepest gratitude to Axel Vervoordt for the trust he has placed in them since the publication of *Timeless Interiors* more than a decade ago.

They extend the warmest gratitude to Michael James Gardner, with whom they have immensely enjoyed working from the inception of this truly original book.

Thanks also to Anne-Sophie Dusselier and to all of the contributors who participated in the text development and photographic research.

Credits

The publisher has made every effort to identify the rights holders for the works of art and photographs reproduced in this book and will gladly correct any inadvertent errors or omissions in future editions.

Copyright for the Illustrated Works

p. 177, 181, and 183 © Jef Verheyen / ADAGP, Paris, 2017; p. 191 © Günther Uecker / ADAGP, Paris, 2017; p. 215 © Kazuo Shiraga; p. 219 © Fujiko Shiraga; p. 221 © Saburo Murakami; p. 223 © Lucio Fontana / ADAGP, Paris, 2017; p. 237 © Dae-Sup Kwon; p. 243 © Sadaharu Horio; p. 247 © Raku Kichizaemon XV; p. 249 © Shiro Tsujimura; p. 267 © Anish Kapoor / ADAGP, Paris, 2017; p. 279 © El Anatsui; p. 281 © Anish Kapoor / ADAGP, Paris, 2017

Photographic Credits

p. 4 © Congo Blue; p. 13 © Vervoordt family archives; p. 15 © Vervoordt family archives; p. 21 © Jan Liégeois; p. 25 © Jan Liégeois; p. 29 © Vervoordt family archives; p. 37, 41 © Congo JC; p. 51 © Laziz Hamani; p. 57 © Frederik Vercruysse; p. 61 © Jan Liégeois; p. 65 © The Metropolitan Museum of Art, New York, Purchase, Friends of European Sculpture and Decorative Arts Gifts, 2000, www.metmuseum.org; p. 77, 79 © Kees Hageman; p. 81 © Jean-Pierre Gabriel; p. 85 © Foto Berben; p. 87 © Pamela Hanson; p. 95 © Axel Vervoordt company archives; p. 101 © Pamela Hanson; p. 105, 107 © Axel Vervoordt company archives; p. 113 © Congo Blue; p. 117 © Georg Fischer; p. 119 © Fritz von der Schulenburg / The Interior Archive; p. 125 © Michael Paul; p. 129 © Bernd Urban; p. 133 © Axel Vervoordt; p. 141 © Jean-Pierre Gabriel; p. 143

© Congo Blue; p. 149 © Fritz von der Schulenburg / The Interior Archive; p. 153, 155 © J. Paul Getty Museum, Digital image courtesy of the Getty's Open Content Program, www.getty.edu; p. 159 © Laziz Hamani; p. 165 © Archives Landau; p. 167 © Laziz Hamani; p. 169 © Congo Blue; p. 173, 177 © Jan Liégeois; p. 181 © Kees Hageman; p. 183 © Serge Korniloff; p. 187 © Laziz Hamani; p. 191, 195, 203 © Jan Liégeois; p. 207 © Axel Vervoordt; p. 215 © Jan Liégeois; p. 219 © Ashiya City Museum of Art and History; p. 221 © Congo Blue; p. 223 © Laziz Hamani; p. 225 © Axel Vervoordt; p. 229 © Jean-Pierre Gabriel; p. 231 © Frederik Vercruysse; p. 235 © Bien-U Bae; p. 237 © Moon Dukgwan (Lamp Studio); p. 241 © Laziz Hamani; p. 243 © Sebastian Schutyser; p. 247 © Takashi Hatakeyama; p. 249 © Mattijs Visser; p. 253, 255 © Vervoordt family archives; p. 257, 259 © Gerald Dauphin; p. 261 © Jean-Pierre Gabriel; p. 263 © Jan Liégeois; p. 267 © Laziz Hamani; p. 269 © Fritz von der Schulenburg / The Interior Archive; p. 275, 277, 279, 281 © Jean-Pierre Gabriel; p. 283, 285 © Axel Vervoordt; p. 287 © Jan Liégeois; p. 289 © Frederik Vercruysse

Editorial Director: Ghislaine Bavoillot

Design: Isabelle Ducat

English Edition

Editorial Director: Kate Mascaro
Editor: Helen Adedotun
Copyediting: Lindsay Porter
Proofreading: Sarah Kane
Index: David Ewing
Color Separation: Bussière, Paris
Printed in Spain by Indice

Simultaneously published in French as
Axel Vervoordt: Souvenirs et réflections
© Flammarion, S.A., Paris, 2017

English-language edition
© Flammarion, S.A., Paris, 2017

87, quai Panhard et Levassor
75647 Paris Cedex 13

editions.flammarion.com

17 18 19   3 2 1

ISBN: 978-2-08-020336-6

Legal Deposit: 12/2017